Angel on My Shoulder

Divine Life Wisdom from the World's Foremost Angel Experts

Edited by Wendy Gabriel

MALACHITE PRESS

Published by:
Malachite Press
Toll-free: (800) 798-9270
www.malachitepress.com

ISBN: 978-1-59598-062-5
Library of Congress Cataloging-in-Publication
information available on request.

Printed in the United States.

For our beautiful teacher, Doreen Virtue,
and her husband, Steven Farmer—
we love you and appreciate you!
Thank you for all that you do.

Table of Contents

Introduction

Welcome to the first collection of works by an inspirational and extraordinary group of individuals. Each of us is an ANGEL THERAPY PRACTITIONER® or an Angel Intuitive™, certified by Doreen Virtue, Ph.D. A best-selling author, lecturer, and psychotherapist, Dr. Virtue calls herself a "teacher of teachers," and she has taught tens of thousands of people around the world the intricacies of communicating with the angelic realm in the hopes that her students will turn around and spread the word to others.

But our learnings are not limited to the angelic realm; our various areas of expertise and our backgrounds are as rich and complex as the Universe itself. Many of us are also energy healers. We are psychics and mediums. We communicate with animals, we work with psychic kids, and some of us are even "undercover" in the world as teachers, nurses, and even television news anchors. And each and every one of us feels called at a deep, soul level to help others in our own unique way.

As you embark on this literary journey with an open heart, we encourage you to use your discernment. Not everyone's message will resonate with you, and that is fine. Please take what you need from this body of work and release the material that doesn't resonate with you. If you find an author that really "speaks" to you, please feel free to contact that person for further conversation, and to learn more about that author's other work, classes, and readings.

We truly hope that our experiences with the angels will touch your heart, make your life's path a little smoother, and show you how to live your life with an angel on *your* shoulder.

Wendy Gabriel

The soul at its highest is found
like God, but an angel gives a
closer idea of Him. That is all
an angel is: an idea of God.

~Meister Eckhart

KRISTI VAUGHN
PALM SPRINGS, CA

Kristi Vaughn is a gifted spiritual healer and accomplished teacher who works with the angelic realm and ascended masters. Over the past several years, she has helped thousands of people connect with their guardian angels and deceased loved ones in her workshops, private sessions, and television and radio appearances. Kristi teaches the practical application of spiritual and Universal laws in daily life, and she encourages her students to uncover their own abilities to use Divine guidance for healing and enlightenment. She works with Goddess energy to create her beautiful hand-made *Aphrodite Rocks* necklaces. Kristi is an ANGEL THERAPY PRACTITIONER®, certified by Doreen Virtue, Ph.D., and has completed Dr. Virtue's Mediumship Certification and other advanced courses. Kristi is also certified as a Theta Healer and Reiki Master.

She is the author of the upcoming book *The Bridge—Quantum Healing for the New World* and has created a pack of oracle cards based on the book.

Kristi lives with her husband and two sons, along with two Chihuahuas, a German shepherd, a mixed-breed pound puppy, and two adopted kitties in the Southern California desert community of Palm Springs. She's a recovering caffeine addict, and when she isn't seeing dead people and talking to angels, she likes to watch cheesy science fiction movies with her kids and read Harry Potter books. Kristi can be reached through her website www.thelightworkers.com.

Faith, Physics, and Angels

By Kristi Vaughn

F aith has not always come easily to me. Several years ago, I was trudging through life—mediocre job, mediocre marriage, stressed out, spiritually asleep. I was trying to convince myself that this was all there was to life and that this was okay. It wasn't! I was bored, unhappy, and disillusioned.

Then things began to change.

I began to feel the influence of my angels, though at the time, I didn't understand it was angelic inspiration. I was guided to read and study spirituality, angels, reincarnation, mediumship, and other esoteric subjects—topics that, at the time, were just plain weird, but fascinating.

Being a student of metaphysics became my pastime. The weird topics began to make sense! It felt as if I was *remembering* the material, instead of learning it for the first time. I wasn't really sure why I felt so compelled to study, but I just knew I had to. What I did know—with astounding conviction and a faith that I had never experienced before—was that this was my mission in life. I had stumbled upon my life purpose. Before I started studying, I didn't even know I had a life purpose! Today I know that the seemingly accidental journey was no accident at all. It was the influence of my angels, with their gentle, loving guidance, pointing me in a new direction.

> Before I started studying, I didn't even know I had a life purpose!

About six months into my crash course in metaphysics, I was guided to study the energy healing modality of Reiki. At the time, I had not discovered my angels; I just had this deep feeling that I was meant to be a spiritual healer. I felt unworthy for this calling, however; I felt unprepared and very much like an imposter. Frankly, the whole thing freaked me out. I believed I had no qualifications whatsoever to be a spiritual healer. I shared my fears and insecurities with a girlfriend, and to my horror, she asked me to do Reiki on her—before I had taken my first class! She'd had a painful and debilitating hand injury, and she would not take no for an answer.

In Reiki training, one is "enabled" to do Reiki through the Reiki attunements during the first class. In theory, one cannot perform Reiki until one has had the attunements. Since I had yet to attend a Reiki training course and had never been enabled through an attunement, I didn't have a clue what I was going to do. But I did feel guided to work with her, so I agreed to try.

The day before I was to meet with my friend, I prayed fervently, like I have never prayed before. My intention was to be an instrument of God, to be a facilitator for both healing and the highest good in the situation. Not knowing what else to do, I wrote down my intentions on a piece of paper and prayed some more. I figured I had nothing to lose.

When we finally sat down together, I prayed and stated my intentions out loud. I laid my hands on her injured hand. Then a very bizarre thing happened. My hands became very hot and very red, and both of us could feel the heat and healing energy surge through my hands. I was doing Reiki, with no training, no attunements, and no conscious idea of what I was doing! My hands stayed hot and red for several hours after I stopped working on her hand, which was rather alarming—I didn't know how to stop the flow of the energy! Eventually we laughed about it together, as it was such a peculiar, surprising experience. My friend's hand felt better after we were done, and she reported back to me a few days later that it was much improved.

What in the world was this all about? I asked myself. It was an exhilarating but confusing event. Soon afterwards, I got an answer to my question. I sensed that this event happened because God (and my angels, although I didn't know it at the time) wanted to get my attention in a dramatic fashion. Well, it worked! It was a startling and life-changing experience designed to demonstrate to me the power of prayer, intention, and faith. In that moment, I got all the confirmation I needed that I was meant to be a spiritual healer. This was the first of many lessons in faith that have changed my life.

The next few years were not easy, but they were amazing. I attended every psychic development class I could. I read every metaphysics book I could get my hands on. I found myself taking what I was learning and putting it into practice as a spiritual healer. I began to communicate with the angels in earnest, opening to the guidance of the archangels and ascended masters, and communicating with spirit guides and deceased loved ones, as well. Eventually I felt urged to step out of my cozy comfort zone and do spiritual intuitive readings for clients—a frightening experience for me because I felt so insecure about my psychic abilities.

It was extremely disconcerting to my family and friends that I had begun talking to angels and seeing dead people. They did not understand. It was even more bewildering to me when my angels guided me to teach others what I had learned. Just when I got comfortable with what I was doing (seeing dead people and talking to angels), here they were again, this time more pointedly pushing me forward, telling me to teach people how to meet their angels. They nudged me to do readings for groups—now I was supposed to see dead people and tell the entire room about it!

It took a tremendous amount of courage to work through my fears, though I constantly felt the loving, guiding hands of my guardian angels. The consternation of my loved ones weighed heavily on me. During this time, there was significant upheaval in my personal life. My marriage had unraveled to the breaking point. Relationships are complicated, and mine with my husband was certainly no exception. My metaphysical studies and work with angels had created tension and misunderstanding between us, and was one of many reasons our marriage had disintegrated. After much prayer, many counseling sessions, and more tears than I care to remember, I came to the devastating decision that the marriage could not be saved.

When I broke the difficult news to my husband, he asked me to stay and continue to work on healing our marriage. I was prepared to tell him no, until he added this: "If you choose to leave this marriage, you are not taking my sons away from me. You will have to move out of the house. They are staying with me. I cannot live without them." That was not the response I was prepared for! Our children meant the world to both of us. He was (and still is) a terrific father, but I had never dreamed he would insist on having physical custody of them. At that moment, I wasn't willing to agree to that. What kind of mother would leave her children?

What happened next is something I will never forget. My angels very clearly and calmly told me, "This is how it is supposed to be. Have faith. Everything will work out fine." Though I could feel their unconditional love and support for me, I was stunned. I was sad, afraid, and angry. Even if the angels were right, I wasn't ready for that outcome. I told my husband I would stay and we could continue to work things out.

My angels had just told me it was okay for me to leave my children! It was *not* okay with *me*! I didn't for a moment believe that things were supposed to happen this way. This incident prompted my first argument with my angels. Speaking from experience, angels are hard to argue with! Their faith is unwavering, and they see the truth where we may be blinded by fear. Their truth is God's truth—beneath our illusion of seeming chaos and drama, all is well, all of the time. As the months passed, I eased back into a place of trust and peace, and I could see that they were right. They had always guided me with love and patience, and I knew they would continue to do so.

The situation played out exactly as the angels had indicated it would. Ironically, this was one instance where I had no doubt that I had heard my angels' message clearly. At the time, I simply did not want to believe or agree with what they had told me—I let my fear outweigh my faith. My husband and I worked very hard to save our marriage for several more months, but it became clear that we could not breach the divide that had come between us. With time and the love and guidance of the angels, with many prayers and courage that surprised me, I came to terms with the circumstances. My soon-to-be ex-husband would keep the kids and the house, and I would strike out on my own. Faith had not completely vanquished fear, but it had changed the way I saw the situation, allowing me to move forward and make decisions about what steps to take. Even when I was afraid, I knew my guardian angels were loving, supporting, and taking care of me.

We had to break the news to our precious children. We faced the difficult task of telling our parents and our friends. I had to leave the home I had lived in for years and find a new home, as well as learn to cope with living in a different household than my children. I had to face the judgment of family members and friends who didn't understand why I left my children with their father. And of course, both of us were left to begin healing our broken hearts.

The challenges in my life at the time were daunting and by far the most difficult circumstances I had ever experienced. And they were a most remarkable lesson in faith. Throughout the entire experience, I relied on the comfort and support of my angels. I envisioned success and prayed about the outcome daily, despite the moments of fear and unknowing. In the weeks after I had moved out on my own, I sat alone and bewildered in my living room. I cried myself to sleep each night. Those were the moments when it felt like faith was the only thing I had to hold on to.

Each morning, I started over again, wiser and a little more optimistic, knowing that I was one day closer to feeling whole again.

Though I was in complete disbelief when I heard my angels' message, they were correct: "Everything will be okay. This is how it is meant to be." My ex-husband and I spoke to each other about the kids regularly and remained on friendly terms. My children and I saw each other all the time, which was truly a blessing.

A close family member told me that I was ruining my children's lives with the actions I had taken. I refused to let her doomsday predictions about my children's future influence me. I have learned that sometimes we walk in faith, knowing that others will question, fail to understand, and make judgments. My faith led me to believe that my children would be fine. They thrived despite the divorce. All of our broken hearts began to heal, because we believed they could.

In the Bible, Jesus tells a group of blind men as he is healing them, "As is your faith, so it is done unto you." (Matthew 9:29) My experience with what Jesus has to say about faith is just that—if you believe it, you will see it. I teach my students about what I call "the assumption of success"—in any endeavor, assume success as the only outcome. The prayer I use is "God, please give me this or something better." Every prayer is heard and answered, even if the answer is no! In my faith, my assumption is that I will only achieve the best outcome, whatever the answer may be.

Yet this understanding of faith was only part of the lesson. There was much more to come. I began to see my prayers and visualizations come to pass, in astonishing detail. For example, when I needed to move, I asked the "real estate angels" for assistance. My wish list of what I was looking for was very specific. I requested an older Spanish-style home with a newer kitchen, tile or wood floors, lots of character, a view of the mountains, nice neighbors, a beautiful green yard (rare in the desert where I live), and a great big bathtub. I was quickly drawn to a place that was exactly what I had asked for. As my desires manifested into reality, I understood that I had created this reality with the power of my prayers and thoughts. That was a very compelling realization!

> Every prayer is heard and answered, even if the answer is no!

About this time, my angels once again directed me to study books I had already read. I had read these books a few times, each time gaining a greater understanding of the information, which had a profound effect on me. As I read them again, I found new lessons about spiritual laws and how they governed us, both in Spirit and in our third-dimensional earthly existence.

While deep in studies of spiritual law, I had my second major argument with my angels, a real doozy. What prompted the argument? I had just taken a weekend course to learn Theta healing and was contemplating why I was struggling so much with the concepts. Theta is a fantastic healing modality, yet it seemed complex and awkward to me. I considered myself an advanced student of metaphysics at this point, but I just couldn't get a good grasp of it. The conversation went something like this:

Me: "Okay angels, help me out here. Why is this so hard for me? It seems so complicated, and yet I know it isn't. It is just out of my reach. What am I missing?"

Them: "We suggest you study physics. Understanding the laws of physics will greatly help you understand the issues you are questioning."

Me: "Physics? What?!?"

Them: "Quantum physics. Albert Einstein. Wormholes. Entanglement theory. Study all of these things, and you will understand how and why quantum healing works, and the relationship between physical and spiritual law. And you will be soon teaching others about this relationship."

Me: "You guys did not just tell me I need to study physics! Not just physics, but quantum physics! Do you know who you are dealing with here? I have college degrees in sociology and art history. You can't get much farther away from physics than the history of art! What are you thinking? Whose idea was this anyway?"

Them: "This is much easier than you think it is. Humans make things so much harder than they have to be. You will find the answers you are looking for when you study quantum physics."

Me: "You have got to be kidding me! I barely passed the 'math for liberal arts majors' course when I was in school."

And so on.

I think most people can understand why I was so upset. Mathematics, science, and most certainly quantum physics, were simply not on the agenda for me, in college or later in life. So, of course, I argued with my angels. This "conversation" happened when I was driving on the freeway. I actually looked around the car and thought to myself, *Who are they talking to?* Because I was sure they weren't talking to me!

At the time, I could not see how this was connected to my work as a spiritual healer and teacher. My angels assured me this was part of the necessary study program and that I would be teaching this to others. Though I disagreed, I listened to them. Part of my lesson in faith has been an understanding of what I call "linear learning." You start at Point A, and then you are shown Point B, then Point C, and so on, until you get to the end of that project or lesson. Then you start again with the next lesson. If we started at Point A and could see all the way to, say, Point M, most of us would throw our hands in the air and give up because it is too overwhelming. By teaching us in baby steps, we are able to handle the lessons, a little bit at a time. Faith is trusting that what you are guided to do today will be the first step in what you are guided to do tomorrow.

I didn't have a clue where to go to learn about physics. But, as I had learned from experience, I put my faith in my angels and

> Faith is trusting that what you are guided to do today will be the first step in what you are guided to do tomorrow.

trusted them to show me Point A. I quickly discovered *Einstein for Dummies* and *The Complete Idiot's Guide To Theories of the Universe*. The concepts within these books weren't easy to grasp for someone who had never been introduced to physics. Thank goodness both books are written for the physics novice!

Faith is the only reason I have pursued the study of physics, which has tested my patience at times! My studies have certainly helped me to grasp what I need to know about physical law and have shaped my understanding of the connections between physical and spiritual law. And just like the angels told me, I am beginning to teach others about what I have learned.

Following the guidance of my angels and surrendering to faith has become second nature, even when I cannot see the reason for what I am being guided to do. I am not sure what my life will look like tomorrow, or five years from now. But along the way, I am enjoying more gratitude, joy, and peace, along with less stress and uncertainty, than I have ever experienced before. The last several years have been an amazing and wondrous journey. And I am willing to bet they were not half as interesting as what is to come!

LAUREL BLEADON-MAFFEI
LOS ANGELES, CA

Laurel Bleadon-Maffei, MA, is an intuitive and channel for the angelic realms.

Joyful, loving, and magnetic, Laurel is a teacher's teacher who is here to inspire Lightworkers to step forward into their life mission. She firmly believes many people are here to "uplevel" the vibration of loving on the planet, creating the next shift in the evolution of human consciousness.

Through workshops and one-on-one sessions, Laurel holds a big space in which people can experience transformation. She assists her clients in attuning to their own divinity, creativity, and magic.

Laurel holds a master's degree in Spiritual Psychology from the University of Santa Monica. She is an ANGEL THERAPY PRACTITIONER®, trained by Doreen Virtue, Ph.D. Laurel also studied mediumship under Virtue, who is a best-selling author, teacher, and psychologist.

Laurel lives in Los Angeles, California, with her beloved husband, Wes, and in the energetic company of her many angel guides, teaching their key message for everyone—"to live in God's dream of us."

Laurel's website is www.illuminatingsouls.com.

The Art of Allowing Transformational Change

By Laurel Bleadon-Maffei

As our soul awakens to its own magnificence, we are often guided to make changes in our lives. Big changes. Changes that seem to upset the apple cart. This chapter is about walking through such transformation. The angels want you to know that when the call comes to change your life, these changes are not made in solitude. There are always many angels and guides sent to help you with the shifts.

In my practice as an intuitive and a channel for the angelic realms, I often work with clients who are going through major transformation. Their dreams are calling them to step forward in new expressions of life. Many of them are Lightworkers awakening to their souls' purposes. After living rather "ordinary" lives, they are finding themselves called to greater levels of service. Their intuitive and mystical gifts are getting stronger. They are on a quest of seeking clarity, understanding, and amplification of their Divine guidance. There is a reason for this. As Lightworkers, many of us are being "activated," and we are reconnecting with our spiritual essence—we are divine ambassadors here to help shift the consciousness of the planet.

I, too, have moved through such a journey. In my late thirties, I found myself working in a corporate job that didn't make my heart sing. I was unmarried, living paycheck to paycheck, and everything in my life felt a little bit beige. It was a time when I was uncomfortable in my own skin and I wished I could change lives with someone else. It felt as if I was just existing, biding my time until I could make it to a ripe old age and gracefully depart this life.

One day, I pulled a card from the *Osho Zen Tarot* deck. The card I selected was the "Celebration" card. It contained the image of three women dancing in the rain under the trees. Their hands and heads were thrown up in exaltation, and they were clearly expressing authentic joy. As soon as I saw the card, I began sobbing. It had been an eternity since I had felt such exquisite joy, and I was utterly homesick for it. It felt as if my soul had forgotten the way. And so I sent a prayer up to God. I asked, "God, please show me how to live my life from that place. I don't know how to get there." With that prayer, I gave God and the angels permission to help me heal and transform. With that prayer, my healing journey began in earnest.

I could fill an entire book about all that transpired on my own journey of healing; there were miraculous moments, leaps of faith, and beautiful friends who helped me find my way. Now, it is a few years later and I have navigated profound transformation in my life. I have left my corporate job for a full-time practice as a channel for the angelic realms (something that I didn't even know I could do until a few years ago!) I have met my Beloved, and we are now married and sharing our journey of light. And I wake up in the morning utterly grateful to be in my life. I no longer want to be anyone else…because I love my life. My prayer has been answered.

If you have been experiencing a rumbling in your soul telling you to wake up, please listen. You may be asked to walk through big changes and profound transformation, but they are gifts sent to help you birth into a life of authentic fulfillment.

What follows are some tidbits of wisdom brought forward to help you on your own path of transformational change. Welcome to Destination Transformation….

Ask God to Show the Way

Earlier, I shared that I prayed and asked God to show me how to live my life in joy. Please ask God to help show you the way. Prayer opens up a powerful portal and allows divine assistance to come streaming into our lives. Contrary to what many of us have been taught, there is no protocol for praying to God. Just open your heart and ask.

This or Something Better for the Highest Good of All Concerned

This phrase serves as a powerful reminder from Spirit that whenever we visualize, dream, pray, and ask for an outcome, to always release it with the caveat of "This or something better for the highest good of all concerned." When we allow for this possibility, it serves as a reminder that we are surrendering this up to God. And we know that only that which is for the highest and best will transpire.

Ask the Angels for What You Need
(It's Okay to be Specific)

When you are moving through change, ask the angels for help. One of the rules for working with the angelic realms is that they are not supposed to help us unless we ask. No matter how big or small the request, just ask. The angels are waiting for you to give them guidance as to how they can best help you. It's okay to let them know what you need in order to navigate the change. For instance, if they are guiding you to leave your job to launch a new endeavor, you can let them know that you need a nest egg of X-number of dollars in order to tide you over until the new business is financially viable. (I used this one on my own journey...and it worked!)

There is an Abundance of Angelic Help

When I teach people about asking the angels for help, there is almost always a pause, and I know they are wondering if their request might be too trivial for the angels, especially when there are so many people in need. It is important to remember that there is an infinite supply of angelic assistance. Just because you ask for help with a seemingly trivial matter, it does not mean that a child on the other side of the world will go hungry. This can be a challenging concept for people to take in, so here's an analogy to help make the point. Imagine going outside and drinking in as much sun as you can. Imagine putting solar panels on your home and allowing them to help fulfill your needs. As you do this, does it feel as if you are depleting the sun's energy? Does it feel like there might not be enough sun for others? Probably not. Rather, you are probably filled with awareness that there is an abundance of sun for everyone's needs. Well, dear ones, God's love and goodness is more expansive than the sun. You can ask for help for anything. The supply of angelic assistance is more infinite than the sun. Asking the angels for help is like putting solar panels on your home. It's working smart.

You are Enough for this Journey

You are enough to make it through to the other side of change. Sometimes change can feel so big and out of reach. God never places a dream in our hearts without giving us all the resources we need to birth it into the world. Remember who you are—a Divine spark of God, sent to help usher the world into a new tomorrow. Of course you are enough for this transformation.

Change Marks the Gateway to a New Adventure

Remember, when change appears, it is signaling that a new expression of our lives seeks to be born. It can be as simple as clearing out a closet or as profound as moving across the country. Change is a tangible and palpable energy that lets us know that Spirit is asking us to grow. Honor change. Make friends with it. Allow it to whisper its secrets to you.

Your Dreams are God's Dreams

The dreams that are breathing through your heart are dreams delivered by God. They are God's way of urging you to a new expression of life. So often, we believe that dreams are what we ask of God. But in truth, they are gifts God asks of us. So allow your dreams to take flight. You are ready. Jump in with both feet, and trust in your magnificence.

Be Selective in Your Support Team

This can be a tricky one. As you navigate change, be selective about who you choose to support you on your journey of transformation. Most people mean well. They do. And they love us. It's just that they might not be the ones who are best suited to help us find our way through major transformation. For instance, let's say you are contemplating buying a new home. You may feel called to share with all your friends and family about your new passion. You're expecting them to rise up and cheer you on. But instead you get a lot of lectures about the dismal state of the economy and interest rates. It has the potential to take the wind out of your sails. Instead, be selective about the people with whom you share your transformational plans. Choose those who will support you...those who see the potential promise in the world. Ask the angels to help you with this. Newly born dreams can be tender and need to be treated gently until they can grow deep roots.

Ask Your Future Self for Guidance

Healing and guidance can travel across time and space. Some-where out there is the you that has already navigated the change. Imagine it... Picture yourself out there in the future, already comfortable in your new life. Then ask your future self how you got there. Ask them for advice. One way to do this is to go into a quiet space and ask your future self to come forward. Then imagine yourself writing a letter from your future self. I did this during a tender part of my journey, and my future self wrote back:

My Dear Sweet Girl~

You want to know how I got here, and I wish I could tell you that it was easy and I flew on the wings of angels. And for parts of my journey, I was carried indeed. But much of it required hard work and pushing far beyond my fear and comfort. For things come easily to us…and then we hit a challenge; and because we are so used to grace and ease, it is not always easy to push beyond the walls that feel difficult and scary. Because in the past, this is where we have given up. But I got here by pushing past that point. Pushing past it and walking through fire.

And so I ask you, are you willing to walk through fire for yourself? Because I was. I walked through fire and blasted through mountains of fear and discomfort for you, my sweet girl. And now you are being asked to do the same. You are going to have to work for this. And I know you are feeling tired and depleted right now, but there are waves of energy and strength and joy that you have not even begun to use.

So breathe and rest and pause right now. But do not tuck away the dream, for it will continue to fuel your heart and show you the way.

And I am here. Waiting for you in the life of your dreams.

When I received this message, I cried, for I could feel that there was a part of me that had already made it safely to the other side. So if you are in the midst of transformation, hang in there. Somewhere out there, you've already made it safely to the other side. Let that energy carry you forward.

Surround Yourself with Light-Conscious Communities

It is not always easy to hold the light on our own. One of the most supportive things we can do is to connect with places that have the highest vibrations of light where we can take a deep breath and replenish our energy. I have been blessed to find such places in Unity churches, hiking in nature, spiritually-based classes, and online communities. We are not meant to navigate through life alone. Allow yourself to receive loving support, and let others pray with you. Truly, it helps.

A Message from the Angels

Precipice of Change

Right now, you are standing on the precipice of change. And right now you may be feeling that it might be too much for you. But it is not too much. It is just the right amount to get you where you need to be. You may be feeling that the change is so big that it will swallow you up. But it will not. It is here to birth you into a new dimension of you that has yet to exist.

Sometimes a part of our old lives must die so that for a time we will stand empty and ready for the new to be born. We stand naked and afraid that this is all there will ever be. But do not despair, dear one. For you are standing on the great chasm between what has been and what will be. You are being called to create a new landscape to your life.

This journey is blessed and paved with both laughter and tears. They are both needed to give our lives depth. Do not fear getting lost, for you are being Divinely blessed as you navigate this uncertain territory. For it only feels uncertain, there is a part of you that has already made it safely to the other side. And it is standing there, lighting your way home. You will not be the same person when you reach the shore, you will be forever changed. Forever more yourself than ever before.

Birth can be painful. It can feel like certain death as we are being squeezed out of a place that no longer fits us. It can feel like darkness is all around us and we are blind to what awaits us at the end of the journey. But know that loving hands are waiting. And the light is bright on the other side. Breathe in the change, dear one. Do not struggle against the building tide, for it will only serve to make you weary. Relax and release your grip on the old. Your new life awaits.

You are standing on the precipice of change. And a bright golden light is shining your way through the darkness. Follow it, for it is leading you home. Home to your heart. Home to your creativity. Home to your love. Home to your courage. And we are cheering you on. You are always surrounded by love. Always.

Affirmation:

With every breath and action, I am creating the life of my dreams. I am willing to change, and to allow change into my life. For I am always remembering that I am safe; it is only change.

(Note: "I am safe, it is only change" in the last sentence was written by Louise Hay.)

NANCY LENNON
BRAINERD, MN

Nancy Lennon is a certified ANGEL THERAPY PRACTITIONER®
with advanced training, taught by Doreen Virtue, Ph.D. She is also a
Reiki Master/Teacher. Nancy took basic and advanced animal communication
classes with author Penelope Smith. Nancy has been providing Reiki sessions
for eleven years, and providing angel readings and workshops for over six
years. Nancy's practice in Brainerd, Minnesota, includes Reiki for pets and
horses, along with intuitive animal communication for individual clients, horse
stables, and vets. She offers classes and workshops about angels and about
animals.

To contact Nancy, visit her website www.rainbowlightangel.com or send an
e-mail to nancy@rainbowlightangel.com.

Animals and Angels

By Nancy Lennon

There are many people in the world who feel deep loneliness. There are moments of feeling separate—separate from nature, from each other, from the spiritual world, and at times, from God. Yet in truth, God has sent many angels to love, support, and watch over us on the earthly journey. But we can't always touch and see the angels among us.

Animals are a source of God's love that we can touch and see. I believe God has sent us animals to fill our hearts with unconditional love. When we hug a soft, fuzzy puppy, feel a cat purr next to our heart, or look into the magnificent eyes of a horse, it helps heal feelings of being separate from our Source. In these moments, our hearts open and fill with love, and we know we are not alone, ever.

There are special animals who are angel-like in their roles to love, teach, and protect us. Their very physical presence allows us to feel connected in our hearts once again. Animals are not angels with big white wings, but there are those who seem to be on special assignment from God.

Angels for Animals

I learned animals have angels who watch over them. The night I had this revelation, our older horse, Blackie, had a blocked and twisted intestine. Blackie had been with us for several years, taking us on many trail-riding adventures. He was a friend. Our choices were to put him down or give him a strong painkiller and pray. I looked into Blackie's eyes and prayed for guidance. His eyes seemed to ask for a little more time. And I knew if it was his time to go, he wanted to be outside in the pasture with his horse buddies. I told the vet to do what he could for Blackie's pain.

The vet gave Blackie a shot for pain, but warned us he probably would not make it through the night. We put Blackie in the pasture with his buddies and prayed some more. At 4 a.m., I woke up suddenly. Something had happened. I saw angels of light surrounding Blackie and felt a sense of peace wash over me. It was like a dream, but I was awake. I pinched myself. Yes, I was awake. Had the angels come to help Blackie die or to help him heal? I just felt a deep sense of peace. Either way, I knew Blackie was not in pain anymore.

As soon as daylight came, I walked towards the pasture. To my surprise, Blackie came running up with the other horses and started to eat. He looked fine. I called the vet later to tell him the good news. He was shocked. The vet had expected Blackie to die and said his recovery was a miracle. He didn't know of any other horse whose intestine untwisted by itself—only surgery had worked, in his experience. I knew the vision of the angels with Blackie had been real. Blackie's survival was truly a miracle.

Blackie recovered completely and is still healthy several years later. He is a miracle horse who helped teach me about angels for animals. He is now helping me with a baby horse that is blind in one eye. But that is another story.

Magic's Sunlight Ripple is a young horse, golden colored with a silvery-black mane and tail. About a week after he came to our farm, I noticed a white spot on his eye. The vet examined it and determined his eye had been punctured. We tried everything to save his eye; we used medicine, Reiki, and a lot of prayers. But eventually Ripple's cornea ruptured, and he became blind in his left eye. At first I was angry with God and the angels. Why weren't our prayers answered for this beautiful baby horse? Where was Ripple's miracle?

Ripple was awkward and frightened in the beginning, bumping into things on his blind side. I noticed in the pasture that Blackie started staying close to Ripple, allowing him to keep his blind side by Blackie. It seemed Blackie was helping to protect Ripple, helping him to feel safe. Eventually, Ripple adjusted by moving his head around to see from his good eye. Ripple and Blackie are buddies in the pasture now. Ripple has become calm and happy again. I realized both Blackie and Ripple were showing me miracles—the miracles of friendship and living life to the fullest. The little golden horse is a blessing indeed!

Ken, my father, shares a miracle story about a wild fox that seemed to have angels watching out for it. Ken says, "Some years ago, when I was a land surveyor, my helper and I were walking through the bush. After about ten minutes of walking through the trees, we came upon a red fox that was struggling in a body trap that threatened to kill it. My helper asked if we should help the fox out of the trap. We discussed how to get the trap open and agreed that I would hold the head of the fox, praying it wouldn't bite me. My helper pried the trap open. The fox walked out of the trap, stopped and looked at both of us, seemed to nod, and walked off into the bush. The 'fox angels' were really working that day."

What are the chances that a wild fox would not bite, especially in a moment of fear and pain? Did the fox understand it was being helped? Did the angels help answer Ken's prayers? I don't know the answers, but I do know something amazing and unusual happened with a wild animal.

Animals and Love

There are animals whose special assignments are to give us love. Ellie is a mini-donkey on my farm. She stands about three feet tall and is a soft gray color. There is a dark brown stripe running down her back and over her shoulders that forms a cross. This is standard for gray mini-donkeys. I can't help thinking about Mother Mary and how a donkey carried her to a stable to have her baby, Jesus. Ellie, the donkey, was pregnant when we bought her. Several people have remarked about how Ellie makes them think about Mother Mary.

When my parents came to visit, I found out just how special Ellie is. My mother, Marlene, was having some health issues and problems with her legs. Initially, walking to the donkey pasture was more than Marlene's legs could handle. After a few days of relaxing at our farm, she decided to try walking to the donkey pasture. When Marlene arrived, the donkeys were excited to see her and came over to visit. Mini-donkeys are very friendly creatures. Marlene's legs felt a little shaky after her walk, and I worried the donkeys might accidentally push her in their excitement to be petted.

Ellie came up to Marlene right away and snuggled up by her legs, as if giving her a hug. I prayed, "Please don't move and push Mom over."

The little donkey stood perfectly still the whole time and her body seemed to help give Marlene support. Ellie also kept the two more rambunctious, younger donkeys away from Marlene.

Marlene felt a special motherly connection with Ellie and said, "There was certainly a lot of love and warmth emanating from her into me. It was not physical warmth, but warmth inside me. It was very special."

Ellie had never bonded so quickly with another person or stood still that exact way. How did she know it was the perfect way to give physical support and love? On the last day, as my parents began to drive away, we saw the three donkeys come up to the pasture by the driveway, as if to say goodbye. (The donkeys had not been to that part of the pasture before.) Marlene remarked, "Ellie and the two younger ones stood quietly and gazed into our eyes as we drove away. That was healing, too. The donkeys touched our hearts with their love, healing support, and gentleness."

Another experience with animals' capacity to love happened in a class I was teaching with a horse called Bobbie. Bobbie had been a school horse for children, including those with special needs. He is an older horse, who is gentle with the children. He is white with brown and black markings. When I first met Bobbie, he was in a lot of pain due to a disease called Cushing's. It made his feet hurt, to the point that he would lift one foot after another to try and ease the pain.

The owner's five-year-old granddaughter, Tali, was especially close to Bobbie. She would come into his stall to brush him and talk to him like a friend. Bobbie was her confidant.

Bobbie's owner was concerned about the amount of pain Bobbie was in. She asked me to check Bobbie and connect with him. I treated Bobbie with a form of energy bodywork called Reiki. I could feel the high level of pain and heat in his body. The owner, with tears in her eyes, asked whether Bobbie wanted to be put down. As I looked into Bobbie's soft eyes, he asked to wait a little longer. The little girl Tali still needed him. The owner discussed the situation with the vet, decided to increase Bobbie's pain medication to the maximum level, and give it one more week. We prayed he would be relieved of his pain.

A few days later, I had a dream about Bobbie. I could see Bobbie up in Heaven, asking God and the angels for a miracle. He wanted more time to continue his mission of healing hearts.

I called Bobbie's owner the next day and told her I had an interesting dream about Bobbie. She said Bobbie's condition had improved overnight. He was eating and walking around with less pain. And he had a twinkle in his eyes again. A few days later, Bobbie was taken off of his pain medication and was much better. Bobbie had received the miracle he asked for.

About a month later, I was teaching a class called Connecting with Horses. Bobbie was the first horse we used as a demo horse. I was leading an exercise with the class to feel the horse's sensory field around their body. Horses have a large sensory field, which allows them to sense any danger. The people in the class walked slowly towards Bobbie, from a distance of about thirty feet away. They had their palms facing Bobbie, feeling for any physical sensations. At about twenty feet, people were feeling a tingling in their palms and stopped. I asked the class partici-pants to close their eyes and feel Bobbie's presence. I felt a strong sense of warmth in my chest and heart. I looked at the class and saw every one of them had tears rolling slowly down their cheeks.

When it was time to share about the experience, the comments were similar: the class participants felt joy, love, warmth, or a sensation of healing in their hearts.

Here was a horse that most of the class did not know, sending an amazing amount of love felt by everyone. Afterwards, I told the class Bobbie's story and the dream in which he asked God and the angels for a miracle to allow him to stay longer. Bobbie had received his miracle and was fulfilling his wish to keep healing hearts. He certainly affected the hearts of all of us in the class.

Many people have their own pets who give them love on a daily basis. When I arrive home after work, our dog Casey wags her tail so hard it makes her whole body move. She is very happy to see me. When Casey sits beside me, she snuggles up close and licks my face as if to make sure I know how much she loves me. It lifts my spirits, no matter what my day has been like.

Learning to Connect With Animals

In the busyness of our regular lives, we enjoy our animals but don't always stop to connect with them on a deeper level. An animal has a day-to-day, regular part of its personality that eats, plays, barks, runs, etc. But an animal has a wise part as well, the part that loves us, understands us, and teaches us. You can learn to consciously connect with the wise part of your pet to learn more about it.

The most important part of connecting on a deeper level is to relax and quiet your mind. Animals are also much more connected to the earth. The exercises which follow will help you become centered and enter the place of stillness, where you can connect with your animal. And the angels will assist you to help it flow easily.

EXERCISE 1: HEART TO HEART

Step1: Grounding
Feel your feet below you, and wiggle your toes. Feel the earth supporting you. Take a few deep breaths, breathing out any stress and worries of your day.

Step 2: Heart Breath
Imagine you are breathing from the earth, up through your feet, flowing into your heart. Do this for several breaths. Imagine you are breathing from the heavens, down through the top of your head, flowing into your heart. Do this for several breaths. Feel your heart open to receive.

Step 3: Ask the Angels

Ask the angels to help you connect with your animal. If you have any doubts or fears, ask the angels to clear them away. For example: "Dear angels, please help me to clearly and easily connect with the heart of my animal, _____." Or: "Dear angels, please clear away any doubts or fears I have about connecting with animals. Help me to clearly and easily connect with my animal, _____."

Step 4: Heart-to-Heart Connection

Close your eyes and picture your animal being with you. Feel your heart connect with theirs. What does your animal's heart presence feel like? Notice any sensations, feelings, or images. You may notice sensations, such as warmth; or feelings, like joy. Simply allow yourself to feel. Trust what you receive and write down your impressions. Practice this exercise with different animals. It is interesting how they each have their own feeling and presence.

At a horse stable with over forty horses, I have had the opportunity to experience many different heart essences. One horse, Joy, is very gentle and sensitive, with a soft heart. Another horse has a warrior-type presence—big, strong, and magnificent. And of course, there is Bobbie, with his wise, healing heart. Each animal has its own personality and feelings, just as people do.

After you feel comfortable with the Heart-to-Heart exercise, it is time to experience even more! Some animals seem to be with us for a traditional reason, like companionship. Then there are those animals who have moments of being wise beyond reason and have a larger purpose for being with us. For example, many dogs have protective roles, as well as roles of companionship. There are other animals that have roles as teachers.

I have a horse, Juna, who is very sensitive. If I walk out into the pasture in a hurry, with my mind racing about the day, Juna will not let me near her. I have learned to take a few minutes to breathe deeply, relax, and clear my mind before visiting her. If I do that, then Juna is fine. I can pet her, put a halter on, or whatever else I need to do. Juna has taught me to calm down and be more fully present in the moment. Her teaching is a gift in my life.

With your own animals, you may already have a sense of their larger purpose in your life. In this second exercise you will be asking the angels to help you connect with your animals and share even more about their purpose.

EXERCISE 2: WISE ANIMAL PURPOSE

First, repeat steps 1-4 of the Heart-to-Heart exercise: Grounding, Heart Breath, Ask the Angels, and Heart-to-Heart Connection. Once you have connected to the heart of your animal, then add the next step below.

Step 5: Connecting to the Wise Self
Ask the angels, "Dear angels, please help me to easily see, hear, feel, or know my animal _____'s purpose for being with me."

Notice any feelings, images, or impressions you receive. If your mind wants to wander, focus on your breathing for a few moments and relax.

Keep in mind the answer can be short, such as "to provide love," or the answer can be more complex. Most often, the purpose will not be a surprise to you, but recognition of something you have thought about or felt. Understanding more about your animal will touch and amaze you. As you practice these exercises, it will become easier and easier to enter a quiet space where you can connect with your animal.

There will still be moments when animals can be frustrating and not wise at all! My dog Casey barks and growls at the UPS man, no matter how many times I ask her to be quiet.

You will start to notice more of the moments when your animal seems to understand from a higher perspective than is rational. And you will be even more aware of the love they give.

Believing

We all need more unconditional love in our lives. The animals that grace our lives give us love with great joy. Although we know that God and the angels love us, the love from animals is tangible and present in our physical lives. It is truly a gift from God.

When we connect with our animals, it helps us believe again—believe in love, healing, and even in miracles. In the moment of connectedness, it can help us believe in a God who cares enough to send animals and angels to watch over us.

SOPHIA FAIRCHILD
LAGUNA BEACH, CA

Sophia Fairchild is a seasoned traveler and writer. Her stories have appeared in many publications, including *Soul Moments*, also published as *Coincidence or Destiny?* (Conari Press, 1997), *Traveler's Tales: Tuscany* (Traveler's Tales Guides, 2001), and *Angels 101*, by Doreen Virtue (Hay House, 2006). Look for her new book, *Soul Wings: Secrets of An Enchanted Life*, coming soon.

Sophia is a certified soul coach, past-life therapist, Interior Alignment® and space clearing practitioner, having personally trained with Denise Linn, author of many best-selling books, including *Sacred Space*. She apprenticed under French Master Sacred Geomancer Dominique Susani in earth acupuncture and sacred geometry. Sophia is also a certified medium, professional spiritual teacher, and an ANGEL THERAPY PRACTITIONER®, certified by Doreen Virtue, Ph.D.

Born in Australia, Sophia now makes her home by the sea in sunny California.

Contact Soul Wings™ at www.soul-wings.com.

From the Mundane
to the Miraculous

By Sophia Fairchild

Introduction

The following three stories reveal how, even at the slightest invitation, compassionate angels and powerful archangels are willing to guide and teach us—eager to bring miracles into every aspect of our daily lives.

The Lost Earring

Angelic miracles, both large and small, are available to everyone. All that is required of us is that we request help, have a little patience, and maintain an unwavering faith that what we desire will become manifest in God's perfect timing. Let go of *how* this will happen. Angels can help us with even the smallest everyday things, like finding lost items.

Not long ago, while unloading groceries in the kitchen, I reached up and discovered that one of my earrings was missing from my ear. My heart sank, as this was my favorite pair of earrings, with many special memories.

I'd bought them from an artisan in the heart of the historical Rocks district in Sydney during a family reunion. The fine hand-worked silver scrolls, intricately woven into the form of crosses with small moonstones at their hearts, instantly caught my eye.

The earrings quickly became favorites; I'm wearing them in all the happy photos taken with my son during that same family reunion.

Now, standing in the kitchen, clasping my nude earlobe, my mind played back over all the places I'd visited that day, scanning for the moment the earring might have slipped off. I'd made several stops at various locations across town, and really, the missing earring could've been anywhere by now.

Not yet ready to abandon hope, I thoroughly checked my hair, clothing, pockets, purse, and shoes. Then, I scoured the shopping bags in the kitchen, retraced my steps back out to the car, then searched inside the car, under the seats, under the car, and even under the trunk mat around the spare tire. Nothing!

I felt so sad to lose one of this beautiful pair. The other earring looked so lonely sitting on my dresser; I couldn't bring myself to put it away. Something told me not to give up hope, even though I felt the lost earring was probably lying on the ground somewhere, possibly in the parking lot of my local grocery store.

I said a prayer to the angels then, to please help the lost earring find its way back to me. I didn't know how this would happen, but I had a feeling that if I had complete faith that the pair of earrings would be reunited, then somehow, miraculously, they would!

The remaining earring sat out on my dresser so I could see and touch it every day, and daily ask that its mate be returned. Every couple of days I'd recheck around the garage floor and entrance to my house in case I'd missed seeing the small earring during my initial search.

Two weeks after losing my treasured earring, I returned from a shopping trip to the same local grocery store. Though I'd not given up hope of finding the lost earring, events over the previous week had replaced my thoughts with more pressing concerns. Still, coming home and unloading groceries in the kitchen reminded me of that lost earring, and I wondered now if I would ever see it again. I finished unpacking the groceries with a sigh and went back through the garage to water the garden.

As I passed by the passenger door of my car, something under the front tire caught my eye. I saw a flash of silver and realized, *There it is! My lost earring!!* I could barely believe my eyes. It was slightly bent and a little the worse for wear, but not in any way damaged!

It appeared to have traveled in between the tire treads and dropped to the ground under the wheel once the car had come to a stop. As I reached down with awe to pick it up, tears of gratitude filled my eyes. "Thank you, angels!" I said aloud and quickly took it back inside to reunite it with its mate. Those earrings hold so many happy memories!

I'll never know what really happened, but it's just possible that I dropped that earring as I was getting into the driver's seat on my previous trip to that store. Then, two weeks later I managed to run over it with my front passenger tire while pulling into the adjacent parking space. Whatever happened, the angels somehow brought my favorite earring back to me, after I prayed to them for help.

I truly believe now that with a little bit of faith, and lots of help from the angels, *anything* is possible!

The Enchanted Forest

Fairies are angelic spirits who live in nature and come in many forms. If we allow them, they will share their ancient wisdom with us, gently guiding us through periods of wilderness in our lives, through those times when we feel lost or alone.

Late one night, on a remote island near Canada, I joined some friends on a vision walk into the forest. The moon had already set and tall trees obscured the stars above, so the darkness was total. There was no wind, and the forest seemed eerily hushed.

The purpose of this vision walk was to train our intuition in preparation for a vision quest and sweat lodge arranged by my dear friend Denise Linn. To vision walk means to walk in nature with reverence, holding the intention of receiving new insight, while remaining open for messages and signs.

In a traditional vision quest, the seeker ventures into the wilderness to sit alone inside a sacred medicine wheel. From the safety of this circle, she goes within to a place of silence, communing with nature and the celestial realms. For three days and nights she calls for a vision, to obtain guidance and direction for her life's journey.

Our small group of friends proceeded silently through the trees, enveloped in the jet dark night. I opened my senses to the mysterious energy of the old-growth forest around us, hoping not to stumble, and praying to see or feel a sign. Now and then a murmur washed over the woods, like a whispered breeze moving through the pines. Yet the forest itself was still. The only movement was our quiet procession forward, deeper and deeper into the forest.

I was beginning to fear I'd lose my footing and fall down in this absolute blackness when I sensed a presence in the trees. A quiver of energy rushed through my body, and I knew we were no longer alone.

Something gently brushed up against me, and the hair on my arms stood up. I sucked in my breath and my heart pounded wildly. I could feel the smooth energy of an invisible forest creature moving along at my side.

My fingertips began to tingle as a soft energy, like champagne bubbles, gradually enveloped them. Instinctively, I turned out my palms. Before I could flinch, the creature had softly taken my hand. The filmy shape of this small wild creature now walked alongside me, guiding me through the darkness with its ethereal light, gently holding my hand.

Other forest creatures were moving amongst my friends. They floated along beside us, around us, and through us. I could tell from the gasps of surprise around me in the darkness that the creatures had also made physical contact with my companions.

The forest spirits had come in a group. They were short—no more than four feet tall—and seemed naked except for the silvery glow that shimmered all around them. Their energy felt like the wisdom of children. These shy, compassionate creatures were now blanketing us in a cocoon of sweet, innocent love and protection.

The forest fairies had joined us!

We walked together in an enchanted silence—the small tribe of forest fairies and my little band of friends. The fairies did not leave us as we paused on the rocky shoreline at the bottom of a hill, where phosphorescence lit up the midnight waters, reflecting the starlight above. They stayed close by, walking silently with us all the way back up the hill, through the dark forest, towards the glowing embers of our campfire, then melted back into the shadows without a sound.

It wasn't until we reached the light of the camp that we finally saw each other's faces. Most of us wept tears of joy. Some were utterly speechless; others openly sobbed. Everyone was amazed at what had just occurred. We had all felt or seen our fairy escorts, moving with us through the woods. A truly heart-opening experience!

Justly humbled by the night's events, we crept into our sleeping bags. That night, I dreamt that the forest fairies were happy and very grateful to us for acknowledging their existence. They had come to guide us through the darkness and purposely revealed their presence so we would know that they are real.

It was exhilarating to go out the next morning and feel their crystal energy sparkling amidst the ancient pines. I looked for their tracks on the forest floor, but the fairies had left none.

And the message from the forest fairies is this:

Never cut down a tree without first honoring it with gratitude for the food, shelter, and fresh air it has provided throughout its life, for all living creatures on earth. Trees also help to bring life-giving rains, anchor the soil, and balance underground water tables. Wherever possible, plant at least two new saplings for every tree felled. The fairies will thank you for this because trees are also their homes.

And the fairy who walked beside me that dark night, holding my hand in the magical silence, taught me that we're never alone.

Just *believe*!

House of the Spirits

Even when we don't know what to do or how to do it, the angels are there to assist us and teach us. This is true even if we aren't aware of the angels' existence. All we need do is request help from the Universe and be open to receiving it. Angels can be our greatest teachers, especially when we're receptive to their instruction.

Many years ago, I bought a ramshackle house on a hill overlooking the ocean. It was badly run down and stood on a street littered with newspapers and broken appliances. But it was the only house I could afford at the time. I suspected something was very wrong with this house when, in spite of its beautiful location and low price range, nobody but I showed any interest in buying it.

Looking back now, it was glaringly obvious what the problem was. At the first and only open house, the few buyers in attendance got no further than the entry hall before the blood drained from their faces. They bolted back to the safety of their cars and immediately sped away. The realtor stood well away from the house, meekly pointing out the ocean views and apologizing that the house had stood empty for some time.

I, too, sensed the cold, clammy atmosphere emanating from the house, but carefully ventured inside. I tried not to blanch at the broken vintage plumbing, holes in graffiti-covered walls, decades-old junk piled up to the rafters in the grim garage, and personal items abandoned in haste, strewn like confetti across the yard. Yet the lovely ocean view and glimpses of what must have been a magnificent garden, now lying buried beneath weeds and trash, gave me some confidence that I could make a thing of beauty from this wreck of a house. And besides, this was all I could afford.

At the auction I was the only bidder, except for a man I suspected was a stooge, positioned there by someone to deliberately jack up the price. Fortunately, I called his bluff and was thrilled to secure the house for a sum even lower than I'd expected. It seemed like a miracle to own my own home at last!

Shortly after we moved in, I began hearing strange stories from my nervous neighbors about the previous residents of my new address. An old woman who'd survived the Nazi death camps had lived there alone for many years before dying in my bedroom. A tormented soul, she took aimless bus rides, crisscrossing the city every day, apparently to get away from someone or something that was always chasing her. It was sad to think she was so frightened of her own home after all she'd been through.

The house had then fallen into disrepair through years of neglect. The last tenants had been a group of occultists who must have enjoyed the nightly parade of ghosts that streamed through that windswept house—until they left in a big hurry! Even my cats knew this house was truly haunted. But I still managed to gloss over this embarrassing detail, mainly because I didn't know what to do.

I enlisted the aid of a Feng Shui expert to begin work on clearing the house of its dank, cloying energy. He dowsed the property and pointed out a couple of powerful ley lines that intersected beneath the house. We hammered copper pipes into the ground across these lines, hoping to calm the energy down, and moved the furniture around in my son's room. Thankfully, his bedroom now had the nicest energy.

When the man had done all he could, he left me with a recommendation to call in a specialist to perform an exorcism.

A what?!

Okay, an exorcism.

But who do I call?

He didn't know. This wasn't something you could dial up from the Yellow Pages, like pizza. I'd seen the movie *The Exorcist*, but had never heard of anything like this happening in real life before.

By then, I was terrified and, not knowing who to call or where to turn, finally began praying for assistance. After this, a very strong image formed in my mind's eye of a stained glass window in an old Gothic cathedral. With nothing else to go on, I decided to search among the dusty shelves of an antique book store for anything I could find on medieval exorcism.

It was there that I happened upon an image that took my breath away. It was an illustration in a thick, leather-bound book of Archangel Michael, taken from a brilliant stained glass panel in an old English church.

Michael is the prince of the heavenly armies…the faithful call upon him in all dangers of soul and body…

… implore his intercession at the hour of death…that their souls may by him be brought before the throne of God.

The fragile gilt-edged book also mentioned prayers for calling upon Archangel Michael's assistance when dealing with *daemons*. I broke out into a cold sweat. This was the nearest I'd come to a description of how to exorcise a haunted house.

The watered-down Christian tradition in which I'd been raised placed no emphasis on the dramatic presence of archangels. As I stood gazing at the beautiful colored image of Archangel Michael, aiming his mighty spear at the terrible dragon pinned under his shoe, I knew I'd found the right man for the job!

Up until that moment, deep down I'd thought that if I ignored the fact that my house was haunted, the ghosts would simply go away. I'd been too ashamed to admit the truth, even to myself, especially since I didn't know how to remedy it. Yet acknowledging there is a problem, whatever it is, is always the first step to resolving it.

I then saw clearly that to deny the existence of the swirling legions that moved at liberty throughout our house each night was utterly futile. I'd been completely helpless and totally out of my depth, but Archangel Michael was now throwing me a lifeline. There was no doubt in my mind that he had led me to this bookstore. I jotted down some notes from the old book, through streaming tears of gratitude.

That night, I got into bed and closed my eyes. My son was away at a sleepover. It was time. The room was icy cold and the whole house was as twitchy and tense as ever. Not sure what to do next, I simply said a prayer to Archangel Michael, appealing for his help. He instantly appeared in my mind's eye as a tall, fiery figure. I actually felt his warmth fill the room and was immediately comforted by his presence.

I asked him specifically to please help me get rid of the ghosts or entities that were in our home. As soon as I mentioned them, I saw, like a movie screen in my mind's eye, a great number of shapes gathering in the darkness before me. Thank God my son wasn't in the house!

Archangel Michael stood in front of me, shielding me with his great wings and huge aura of burning white light. The souls that had gathered before him also seemed calm in his presence. I then noticed that he was directing them to move off to the right where a small opening of light was growing brighter.

It was as if a heavy stone were being rolled away from the entrance to the side of a mountain, and we were all watching from inside a cave as the glowing rays of the sun streamed in to warm us. The golden white light shining through that opening seemed to beckon to the huddled spirits inside. All I could do was watch as Archangel Michael bid them one by one to walk through that door into the brilliant sunshine.

Once the line of shadowy souls began to move towards and through the lighted doorway, more and more kept coming! This procession seemed to go on and on for a very long time, and though I felt myself drifting off, I fought to stay awake to see what would happen next.

The archangel must have sensed my fatigue. He commanded those who had not yet gone through the lighted door to go away for now and leave me in peace. At his direction, they simply melted away. It seemed that Archangel Michael had opened up a portal for all those lost souls to move through, so that they would no longer be restless and stuck in a place they didn't belong. And all this was done without any battle, in the most peaceful, compassionate way.

The energy in our house quickly settled down, and the archangel returned many times to usher these souls away into the light. They seemed to come from miles around whenever he appeared, to stand in an orderly line and move into the light he'd provided for them.

In time, Michael no longer needed to visit so regularly and our house began to feel more like a home. I was later told by a neighbor that the land near the top of that hill was probably once an ancient burial ground. And the house itself stood just a few blocks away from an existing cemetery dating back to the earliest settlers. My son even discovered his great-great-grandparents buried there. Evidently, Archangel Michael had called out to a vast number of souls, including those who'd died centuries before, to move into the light.

Shortly afterward, I met and worked with several indigenous shamans to bless the house and land, though nothing was ever quite as powerful as the work Michael had done during those early, jittery days. The important lesson he taught me was to always allow him to do the work, rather than trying to do it by myself. Without fail, he stood in front of me for my protection. This allowed me to feel perfectly safe and peaceful while these strange events unfolded. We had some very happy years in the house after that.

Much later, after reviving the beautiful gardens and renovating the property with great care, I sold that house on the hill for a record price. And by this time, thanks to Archangel Michael's work, the sound of small children could be heard playing happily in that beautifully restored neighborhood.

LISA GRUBB
SOUTHERN HIGHLANDS,
AUSTRALIA

Since the early 1990s, Lisa Grubb has been an internationally published author and storyteller who is especially well known in the Las Vegas, Nevada, area. Currently, she is writing and offering workshops on material from *A Course in Miracles* in Australia. Working with the *Course in Miracles* since the late eighties has transformed her life and inspired everything that she has done. She shares her story of transformation, life, and inspiration with the world.

Her work has been featured in Doreen Virtue's *Fairies 101*, and in *Spirit Wisdom* (online www.spiritwisdom.com.au) and *Bellus Materia* in Queensland, Australia. Her titles include *Bury Me with No Stone*, *Living in the Lights*, *Wouldn't it be Nice*, and *The Art of Acceptance*. Lisa can be contacted at lisa@divinitydesigns.com.au.

Earth Angels Among Us

By Lisa Grubb

From the moment I entered this world, I walked with the angels. I was born several weeks premature, black from lack of oxygen and fighting for my life. Even in these early moments, I was not alone. Earth angels in the forms of doctors and nurses fought to save my life, and heavenly angels were on the other side, guiding them and helping me heal. The angels have been with me, literally, since birth.

In the beginning, Heaven's angels mainly communicated with me as voices in my head. As a child, I would sit and talk with them; they would surround me and tell me stories. Of course, not everyone was open to hearing the angels' stories—I learned that fairly young. When I mentioned their tales to others, I was quickly told to hush. Such things were simply unheard of; the angels' stories held tales of life unknown to those around me.

My tales held stories of "ladies in the night." Those around me could not imagine where I was coming up with these ideas—they were dismissed as lies, and those around me decided that I lied frequently.

I grew up in a household torn apart by divorce when I was very young. The angels were with me as I faced that difficult transition. I learned to trust in those voices during the really turbulent times, especially when they guided me to escape from the world. I remember feeling relief as I hid, crying in closets or under furniture. At that time, everyone was telling me I was going to have a certain kind of life. Everyone seemed to have a plan for me. But none of their plans fit the person that I knew I was to become. Despite all of the verbal abuse that I endured, I continued to believe in myself. After all, the angels assured me that some day I would "fly above the rest." As people around me tried to fit me into their molds, I resisted, taking comfort in the words of the angels. The angels told me to hold on, to survive; they told me that I was God's child. I was compelled to choose my life's path based not on welfare, but on the road that I felt driven to travel.

Eventually, I was a teenager, old enough to branch out and take a job outside the home. Unfortunately, my first work experience wasn't a particularly good one. When I first started working, I was sexually abused. I dreaded my Saturday morning shifts, for it seemed that every Saturday, I would find myself alone with the owner of the shop, cornered in the basement with nowhere to turn. I would close my eyes as he touched me, blocking out the tears. I knew I had no choice but to endure and pray for the moment to end. Today I would strike back at sexual harassment forcefully, but at the time, I was very young—I had no idea that I had rights. Also, at that time, my job seemed my only escape from my abusive home life. Others would ask me how I managed to avoid harm at work and at home, and I used to laugh and say that I had two guardian angels: one to watch while the other's back was turned.

After years of abuse within my family and on the job, I started the all-too-common pattern of self-abuse. I became bulimic. Food was my comfort, and fighting my weight was turning into a daily battle—eating and purging seemed to answer both needs. By the time I was nineteen, I was a wreck—indulging in every mind-altering substance known to humankind (and a few brought in from the elemental world!)

I was also having sex with whomever I could find to hold me, finding fleeting moments of comfort in their touch. I started stealing, lying to my friends, passing my nights in an alcohol-soaked blur. Today I know that all of these behaviors were simply a means to fill a void within me. I had forgotten that love came from within. This world had taught me that love came from others, but there was no love left for me. I existed in a loveless world. I genuinely hated myself; I wanted to die. I was in real danger of becoming a statistic of teen suicide.

Yet the angels loved me anyway. Their love gave me the strength I needed to make some changes in my life. I left that abusive job, I moved out of the abusive home of my youth, and I tried to stand on my own two feet. I lived in a half-dozen places, never for long in any one spot. Moving with the work, moving when life was too hard to exist. It was extremely difficult, though—all I had ever known was abuse; I did not yet have the inner resources to defeat my inner demons.

Right before my twenty-first birthday, a man I was dating arranged what I thought was a wonderful birthday present—a wild night out on the town. It turned out to be a nightmare.

After this terrible night, my angels gave me an out. They told me to run—run as far away as possible. I listened to those voices, I packed my bags, bought a plane ticket, and flew away into the night. My airplane landed amidst the neon lights of Las Vegas. All I had was a suitcase and fifty dollars in my pocket, but it didn't take me long to figure out how to survive—I became a call girl. Life had already taught me how to endure these kinds of difficult situations. Long ago, the angels had whispered to me about this life, life as a "lady of the night"; now it was my reality. This was my life for the next four years. I had not chosen a path that led up, only sideways. I existed as a creature of the shadows, feeding on the seamy underbelly of Las Vegas. Drugs, booze, sex for money—I forgot what it was like to live in the rays of the sun, what it was like to be truly myself. I stopped listening to my angels completely and surrendered to the life that was set forth by years of sexual abuse.

Four years into my Vegas adventure, I became a statistic in the world of sex crimes. I was working as an escort for one of the agencies in town. The service offered "entertainment"—in my world, that meant sex for a fee. Working with an agency was a means of offering protection. Before the call was relayed onto me, the girls working in the office were supposed to have screened the job. That night, there was no screening. The "client" beat me and raped me at knife-point. As I endured each painful assault, I felt genuine terror—for the first time in my career as a call girl, I honestly thought I would be killed and that no one would know or care. When he was finished with me, he dumped me in an area of town know as the "Naked City." I huddled behind a dumpster, naked and sobbing. My clothes, slashed and ripped, lay in a pile next to me. I still had my purse, but the rapist had stolen everything in it except for a small amount of loose change at the bottom. I put on my shredded clothing as best as I could and limped to a payphone, aching and terrified. I was too scared to call the police—I knew that *I* would be the one to go to jail. I tried to call my roommates for help, but they wouldn't come for me—the night was busy, after all, and there was money to be made.

I had never felt so invisible in my whole life. Finally, after a while, I gathered my wits and remembered that I had tucked a key behind the license plate of my truck. I could drive myself home.

Once safely at home, I tended to my battered body, but my broken heart could not be soothed. It was my darkest moment. I did the only thing that I could think of: I reached out to God and the angels.

"I will follow you!" I pleaded aloud. "You just need to show me how! If this is not love, then what is love? If this is not what life is about, then teach me. Bring me those that I will learn from." As the night passed in a blur of tears, I felt a bright light surround me, bringing me comfort, and with it, sleep.

The sun rose the next day, and as far as I could see, nothing had changed. I was still in terrible emotional and physical pain; my surroundings and circumstances hadn't been miraculously altered during the night. But something had shifted within me—a slight movement, to be sure, but I had created an opening for

Grace to enter. To the Holy Spirit's sight, my world was seeing a new dawn and was being bathed with rays of holy light.

Soon, my living arrangement changed. For too many years, the view from my front window was the back door of a strip club. Life was harsh there, and we existed solely to live and thrive in the night. But then I met a man, yet another one of my earth angels, who would help rescue me from that life. When I first saw him standing in a nightclub, I was drawn to him—I knew we had to meet, that he was meant to be in my life somehow. Of course, I was not conditioned to the ways of kindness or generosity or intimacy—initially, I felt certain that he would probably just be one of my many one-night stands, a customer. Instead, he turned out to be the first stepping stone in my path to a new life. We danced on the first night, "did lunch" the next day, and on the third night, he introduced me to his roommates. Before the week was over I had moved in with them. As I started to live with this new group of people, I knew that I was moving away from my former life of pain. It was time to find a new job. It was time to find a reason to live. It was time to live in the light.

Unfortunately, correcting my course was not particularly easy. A few months after my move, I was still searching for a way to support myself—still looking for a "normal" job. But I was failing miserably in my attempts to exist in daylight. Anything but a nocturnal existence had become a mystery to me! I had to relearn everything that I thought I already knew—how to dress, how to act, how to laugh, and how not to be angry at life. Soon, however, I met the woman who would teach me all of those things, and more.

I was out on a date, and across the room, I saw a woman that I just knew I had to meet. Without hesitation, I walked over to her, introduced myself, put my phone number in her pocket, and told her to call me. The woman I met that night was the earth angel who started me on my true spiritual path, teaching me how to connect with my own inner angel, how to believe in myself, and how to finally soar as I was meant to.

This truly enlightened soul offered me a job working with her as a receptionist at a construction site. From there, the belief others had in me gave me the confidence to learn computer and bookkeeping skills. The work environment that she brought me into was unlike any other I had ever experienced. The people were genuinely friendly and very positive. Everyone was into self-growth, self-awareness, and the power of the holy self. From them, I learned how to overcome many of the demons that I hadn't been able to release. They taught me how to work with my holy light. They suggested I read *A Course in Miracles*. They encouraged conversations that involved information contributed by angelic guides. They taught methods of changing negatives into positives through the use of visualization.

One does not go from the depth of despair to belief in one's self overnight. It took time for my angels—of both Heaven and earth—to teach me self-love, and most importantly, self-belief. By listening to the angels' directions in what to read, what to study, who to talk to, and what to remember, I slowly began to shed the trauma of the years of pain and remember who I really was.

By then, I had been living in Vegas for ten years. My skills as a receptionist and bookkeeper had increased a hundred-fold;

eventually I was in charge of the day-to-day operations of a full-service bookkeeping company.

I'd had so many angels pass through my life that I knew I had to give back. I volunteered for Nevada Cooperative Extension, a program to help youth coming out of foster care adjust to the life around them. I knew how hard it was for me to survive on the streets of Vegas. I wasn't afraid to help anyone, and I told my charges the truth about life on the streets. Soon I was in a position to help a girl that came to work in my office under a work-study program. She was just seventeen; she had been living in a committed institution for children. The teacher at the institute was a friend of mine and had asked me to give the young woman a job and train her. The teen came into the office, shy and unsure of herself, but a willing student, a good worker, and a bright and likeable kid. A few weeks into her work-study assignment, she was given the chance to move back home with her mother and stepfather.

It was a disaster. Her stepfather raped her, and her mother threw her out of the house; her mother said that she could no longer handle the sexual tension that her daughter caused in the home. The state had no option but to put the young woman in juvenile hall, as she was too old to place in a foster home. I was heartbroken that this was the only option for her, so I agreed that she could come and live with me until she turned eighteen. I think that was the first true sign of kindness this young girl had been shown in her life. She stayed with me for several months. We worked on skills such as paying bills, grocery shopping, clothes shopping—simple, day-to-day things that she didn't get to learn while living in the group home.

Things were still very difficult for her, though. She could not release the demons that held her soul, and she tried to kill herself. After that, state authorities put her back into a group home. It looked like a bleak end to a tragic story. I felt like I had failed her. However, it turned out that she was able to make the best of a bad situation. She was allowed to contact her father for the first time in years. He lived in another state and was unaware of how she was being treated. She went to live with him and his family. She finally had a place that she could call home.

I know today I was an earth angel who passed through her life. I didn't like the role I had to play when I discovered her suicide attempt, since I had to return her to her old life within the system; but the angels knew that all I had to do was play a small part in her life—all I had to do was show her love.

Over the next two years, I lived to heal my own pain. I was releasing the demons that haunted me from childhood. I worked continually on forgiveness, filling my mind with positive and affirming beliefs. In the morning, I would offer my services to the Lord. The words "How may I serve you?" filled my prayers. Soon I was asked to serve as an earth angel to another child, this time a thirteen-year-old girl. She followed my dog home. As she sat out on the front walk, petting and playing with the dog, I asked her where she lived. She pointed to the dumpster, and I thought she was pointing to the block of apartment units. I asked if they just moved in, and she burst into tears as she told me how her mother had abandoned her. She was living in the dumpster by my home because it offered her the most shelter.

I took her into my home and proceeded to make the necessary phone calls to notify authorities. Within three days, the child's mother had signed over custody and the little girl became a foster child. During the few months that she stayed with me, I tried to help her understand why her crack-addicted mother had abandoned her. Her world was shattered. Soon she ran away; it was the last I saw of her. The heavens knew she needed a cloud to land on and an earth angel to take her in, if only for a while. Even though I was not looking to be that cloud, my angels knew I was the person for the task.

In healing my broken past, I rediscovered my passion for feeding others. As the angels cleared my soul, I remembered time spent with my grandmother, feeding senior citizens at a Sunday meal program run by our church. As a youngster, I would work alongside her in the kitchen, preparing vegetables and performing other duties. As I grew, I graduated from working in the kitchen to serving the seniors, and eventually, I was committed to the program, performing every task associated with it. Feeding others also proved to be valuable employment; as a teen, my grandmother was the head cook at the local hospital—I only had to ask for a job. As I learned to love myself again, I started to volunteer again, expanding my service to running a holiday meals program for people living with AIDS.

As life changed, I knew it was time to leave Las Vegas. My angels had been telling me for years that when I could see the lights from the mountains, it was time to let go. After eighteen challenging years, I finally saw those lights. I really had no choice. It was time to leave Las Vegas. Life was changing. The angels guided me to my next home, whispering, *"Choose with your heart."* My heart chose Australia; once I'd made my decision, I was supported on the wings of angels.

Eight years later, I was given the chance to realize my life's dream and take over a restaurant. I went with it. Everything seemed to be right, and the move into the new business was effortless. The dream quickly turned sour, though, when the clientele dwindled and the money ran out. In the end, I decided to give up the restaurant. It felt as though my life was crashing around me. As I struggled with abandoning my means of existence, I quietly prayed, "I know you did not offer me this dream to have me fail. Please send your loving angels in to catch me and to lift me up now. If it is your plan for me to stumble, send the angels that will allow me to fall with grace. I forgive this dream of illusion that I have created. All those that played a part in its creation, I forgive, and I release this to your holy light. Send my angels to me now."

After saying this sincere prayer, I quickly fell asleep, secure that the angels were in charge. Within a matter of days, my partner called to tell me she had just won $100,000 by listening to her angels. This allowed us to move on with our lives without negative financial consequences from the loss of the restaurant.

I have to laugh when I remember that just six years before this incident, my partner didn't believe in angels. She actually asked me, "What good is it to believe in them?" At the time of this discussion, we had been driving my four-wheel-drive vehicle on the beach, and we suddenly got stuck in the sand. I didn't let her question—or her doubt—phase me. I simply asked the angels to send help, and she replied, "What good do you think that will do?" I didn't have time to respond, because I was too busy opening my door to four men training for the Ironman triathlon competition coming to our rescue. That was the day she opened her heart to the angels.

It's not easy when you're tapped to be the earth angel with the difficult job. Many people think *Why me?* when they are faced with a moment of pain, a challenging choice of right and wrong, or a seemingly insurmountable problem. The thing I've grown to realize is that *Why me?* isn't the right question—the question really should be *Why* NOT *me?* Why shouldn't you be the one to know God's love or do God's bidding? Why not change someone's life through a simple act of kindness or allow a stranger to change your life?

I spent much of my life wondering why I was here on earth; today I no longer ask that question. We all move in and out of each other's lives, based on what we can teach and what we can learn. The truth is, we are both students and teachers—even when you are the earth angel with the tough life. We exist to offer assistance and to accept and give love; these gifts are based on exactly what we need to fulfill God's purpose for us. To assist us, we have God's gift of prayer; even when you think no one is listening, the angels always hear.

Angels descending,

bring from above,

Echoes of mercy,

whispers of love.

~Fanny J. Crosby

WENDY GABRIEL
MADISON, WI

"Angel Gal" Wendy Gabriel is an award-winning newspaper reporter, a former television news anchor and reporter, and the author of the forthcoming book, *The Kids in the Club* (Malachite Press 2008), a story about psychic children. She is an ANGEL THERAPY PRACTITIONER®, certified by Doreen Virtue, Ph.D., a medium, and a professional spiritual teacher. Besides writing, editing, running her publishing company, Malachite Press, and teaching other how to communicate with their angels, Wendy conducts angel readings with clients around the world.

Wendy is currently compiling a second angel anthology, *Angel on My Shoulder II*, and an anthology of non-fiction fairy tales, as well.

Wendy lives near Madison, Wisconsin, with her two wonderful children, a menagerie of imaginary animals, and a whole bunch of really persistent angels, fairies, and spirit guides. To learn more about Angel Gal Wendy or to schedule a reading, please visit www.angelgalwendy.com, or call her at (800) 798-9270.

Grasping Shadows: Healing Childhood Trauma Through the Angels

By Wendy Gabriel

I was recently diagnosed with attention deficit disorder. Anyone who has this learning disability knows how frustrating and draining it can be. ADD can suck the inspiration right out of you, make it downright difficult to remember even the smallest things, make even the simplest of tasks seem insurmountable. I've dealt with these symptoms and a host of others pretty much my whole life, but up until just recently, I had no idea there was anything physically wrong with me—I just figured that I was depressed, grumpy, and lazy. The diagnosis of ADD was actually an enormous relief.

But it was only a diagnosis. It wasn't a solution. And I wanted to get better! As a writer, editor, publisher, and teacher, I wanted to be of service in a big way, and this disorder was getting in the way. I wanted to push through the difficulties, discover its organic roots, overcome it, move through to the other side, and become well.

So I did what I always do when faced with any kind of challenge. I asked God and His realm of Heavenly helpers for assistance. I sat outside at sunset, feeling the warmth of the spring sun on my skin. I had gone for a long walk a little earlier in the afternoon, reveling in the peace, safety, and serenity of my peaceful Wisconsin community; now it was time for a heart-to-heart with the Universe. I called on my guardian angels for guidance and requested the assistance of the fairies, who are powerful manifestors and healers.

I want to get better! I told them. *I am tired of not getting anything done. I'm tired of the procrastination. I'm tired of the fuzzy thinking. Even though I know that on some level, my soul chose this experience, I'm now choosing something different! Take it away now, please!*

Sometimes when I pray, I can feel the warmth of the angels gathering around me like a comforting blanket, lifting me up and inspiring me. This was not one of those times, however. I sat on that bench, feeling pretty much alone, wondering if anyone was listening.

Just a few hours later I would discover that they had been listening; my request for healing had been heard, and it would be heeded. I never would have imagined, however, that the healing would touch me on so many levels or in such startling ways.

Earlier that day, I'd had an unsettling dream with a recurring theme. In the recurring dream, I was in college. I had returned to the dorms after a long absence, only to discover that I had accidentally forgotten to make accommodations for my goldfish while I was away. When I found it, the poor thing was nearly dead, swimming in disgusting water, starving. In each dream, I would be simultaneously wracked with guilt, shame, and an unidentifiable feeling that made me want to recoil, just disappear.

In past dreams, I had only had one small goldfish in a bowl, sitting on my desk. In my most recent dream, however, I walked into a newer, larger apartment to discover a forty-gallon fish tank packed with a variety of disgusting, diseased, horrible-looking fish. About two-thirds of the water had evaporated, and they were swimming in the fetid, filthy water, bumping against each other, bumping up against the edges of the glass, starving, gasping for breath. The familiar feelings of revulsion, guilt, and shame flooded through me, and I didn't know what to do first— get them food or put fresh water in the tank.

Even though I had experienced this dream for years, for some reason, that most recent dream touched me so deeply that I felt compelled to share it with one of my closest friends, Leisa Machado, in the hopes that analyzing it would make the lingering feelings go away.

As I discussed it with her later that same day, the feelings returned anew, distracting me so acutely that I could barely stand to carry on the conversation. I changed the subject to a lighter topic, but as Leisa talked, I saw a flicker in the corner of my left eye and felt someone join me in the room. I turned around, fully expecting to see my nine-year-old son standing behind me in the basement rec room of our rented home. There was no one there. Yet the energy in the room was palpable. *Maybe I'm just imagining it*, I thought, trying to coax myself back from the terrible funk that was slowly seeping into my brain. But I have been an ANGEL THERAPY PRACTITIONER® and a certified medium for years; I've worked with countless clients and their deceased loved ones. I knew I wasn't making this experience up.

Even as I tried to brush it off, the energy deepened and became more insistent. Despite all of my mediumship training, I had never felt an earthbound spirit so distinctly before. Yet I wasn't nervous—the energy wasn't threatening or angry. I shared what I was experiencing with Leisa and said a quick prayer to Archangel Michael, asking him to carry away any lower energies into the light. The energy in the room shifted a little bit, and Leisa suddenly felt compelled to add, "leaving only the energies that are for your highest and best good."

Then she and I simultaneously "saw" in our minds' eyes a man in his late fifties or early sixties, with short, mostly gray hair and a receding hairline. He was dressed in a white T-shirt, and he was *screaming* at me at the top of his lungs. I couldn't hear his words—I could only see his mouth working furiously as he desperately tried to get my attention. Immediately both Leisa and I knew that this man was somehow tied to childhood sexual abuse. *But why is he bothering me?* I wondered. He didn't look familiar to me at all. I thought perhaps he had sought me out to deliver a message to someone, but since I wasn't currently working with any clients and Leisa didn't know him, his abrupt appearance was a bit of a mystery to me.

I decided to hang up the phone and explore this further. I asked Michael to strengthen the shield around me, and then I settled in for a chat with this "gentleman." That's when the feelings of guilt, shame, horror, and repulsion returned with a vengeance. It was like I had returned to the emotional state that I felt in my dream, only this time, I wasn't dreaming—I was wide awake. I felt him say to me, *I'm sorry for what I did. It was wrong. Everybody knew, but they figured you were so young, that you'd never remember. But I can see that it's affecting you now. That's why I'm here.*

I began to realize that this man wasn't here to give me a message for someone else; he was here to talk to *me*. Tears filled my eyes as he told me that we were members of the same close-knit, conservative church when I was about two and a half years old. The members of this church socialized quite a bit, and they would frequently hold get-togethers at each other's houses on weekends. Apparently, during one of these get-togethers, some-one caught him molesting me. The church elders eventually kicked him out of the church for his actions, although no one ever bothered to call and report the crime to the police. The other adults in the congregation decided that there wouldn't be any lasting harm, since I was so young.

My wife, she never forgave me for that, he told me. He showed me that his shame surrounded him like a black cloud for the rest of his life. He also showed me that even though he had been dead for some time, he had lingered around me. He was now coming forward in response to my call for healing.

At this point, I was quite confused and upset. I knew better than to think that I was just imagining this interaction, but I also felt a little insane. Even though I had always suspected that I had been sexually abused at some point in my life, I had no clear memories of any such event; it had been a very long time since I had prayed for healing in this area. I honestly thought I had released any emotions concerning the possibility of my being sexually abused—what other choice did I have, since I had no memories? But even as I had these thoughts, the angels showed me in my mind's eye the image of me sitting outside earlier that day, talking to my angels and the fairies, asking for help with the ADD issue. Could the two issues be somehow related?

You've asked to be healed, you've asked to be freed from the ties that hold you down. I'm here to say that I'm one of those ties, he explained.

In that moment, I closed my eyes. My brain felt like it was tethered down by a hundred tiny ropes, staked into the ground. Then I was suddenly surrounded by strong, yet gentle, very loving beings—my angels, I knew, and my beloved grandmother. I could feel their love penetrate my body, gently supporting me, even as I began to sob silently.

I want to move through this, I told my angelic helpers. *The only way to survive it is to heal it and move through it.*

As I was talking to my angels, I could "hear" the man in the back of my mind: *I'm sorry! I'm sorry!*

That's when everything started to really come together for me. The feelings from my recent dream were so strong, so revolting, I felt nauseated. The feel of my skin, the taste in my mouth—it was all vile and slimy. I was just a tiny, defenseless little goldfish, left so nasty and dirty and damaged by his actions, I wanted to die; I couldn't even stand to be in my own water. I wanted to disappear; I wanted no part of myself. I wanted to just throw myself out like a dead fish and start over again, to wash out the bowl, and forget it ever happened. But all I could ever do was pretend it never happened. I realized that I was reliving emotions and physical sensations that I had experienced during and after the sexual abuse. At the time, my young brain equated the things I was feeling during the abuse with another incident that happened around that time—the discovery of a dead pet goldfish, floating in foul water. My conscious brain may have forgotten the incident, but my body was holding the emotions and physical sensations in escrow until I was ready to face the incident and release it.

I also saw my young self from the perspective of an adult, a mother, a dedicated defender of children. I could see the damage done to this defenseless child, and I doubled over with the intensity of the pain that I felt for her. I felt as though *I* had failed her. This thought, this feeling, sent fresh grief coursing through me.

Oh, God! How do I heal this? Please! Show me how to heal this! I begged.

Suddenly, I envisioned myself as that tiny, two-and-a-half-year-old girl. I was looking up at that great big man, seeing him through my child's eyes. Only I wasn't afraid, like I was before. As I spoke to him in my imagination, I heard my child's voice in my head, *You're a bad man. You are rough with me, and I don't like it. You're not allowed to hurt me any more. I'm going to tell my mommy!*

I had said my piece, yet he wasn't going away. What did I have to do to get him to go away?

Gramie, angels, please take him away! I half-begged, half-demanded.

I could feel my grandmother flying to my rescue, demanding that he leave—it was almost as though she was just waiting for me to give her permission to have a go at him.

)71(

But the angels held back: I had one task left to complete before he would be free to go.

I had to forgive him.

But how do I forgive him for something that I didn't even know I was hanging on to, for something that I'm still not sure really happened? I wondered, beginning to feel quite drained. I was grasping at shadows, playing games with illusions, trying to scrutinize something that could never be made physical, never be subjected to true scientific examination. Somehow, I had to move on, even though I still wasn't 100 percent sure what I was leaving behind.

Then the angels showed me the man's higher self. The part of him I had been communicating with just moments before seemed almost like a shadow, an echo of the man that he was during his most recent life on earth. But the higher being, the being who was radiant, filled with the love of God—there was no sin in that person, there was no offense. There was only love.

I wanted to feel that love. I desperately wanted to connect with it and therefore return to Source, dissolving this pain forever. But all I could do was acknowledge that it was there, that this man who had come to me, who had apparently harmed me, was but an extension of God. With that acknowledgment, I felt the man begin to pull away from me, his energy rapidly separating itself from mine and dissipating.

He had no sooner slipped away then my attention was directed to the angel that I felt sitting on my right, just in front of me.

"In the effort to suppress things, you became distracted, and depressed, and unable to focus," she gently explained. "These experiences are a byproduct of the forgetting. Suppressing these emotions caused symptoms that are manifesting themselves as the appearance of ADD."

Does getting my head back mean that I have to remember everything that happened? I asked. I didn't think that I could handle that. Still, I felt very strongly that I wanted to heal any traces of ADD. *I want my brain back*, I told her firmly. *I want it to belong to me.*

"Of course you do," she said soothingly. "What you need to realize is that it never went away from you. It just got locked up, a little haywire. It'll get better now."

I mentally called in Michael once again to clear my auric field of any residue from the experience. Yet the emotions of the dream still lingered. I was not done. My gut still felt tender, my eyes still ached with tears. I still felt vulnerable and unloved, despite being surrounded by such loving helpers. As I closed my eyes, I could see my little two-and-a-half-year-old self, alone and afraid. I held out my arms to her and she crawled on to my lap, wrapping her legs and arms around me, hugging me fiercely.

Baby, you're safe now, I told her as I rocked her. *I'm sorry he hurt you and made you feel so bad about yourself. I love you. And I'm never going to leave you.*

Once again, I felt the powerful, warm rush of angelic love surround me as that little girl began to melt into my body, soaking into my energy field, slowly, gradually becoming one with me, finally coming home.

As I think back on this experience, part of me expects Rod Serling of *The Twilight Zone* to step forward and say something like this:

"Wendy Gabriel—middle-aged mother, divorcee, angel talker—healed from a pain that she didn't even know existed by an encounter with a man on the other side of the veil. Such events may seem improbable in the everyday world. But they happen all of the time...in the *Twilight Zone*."

Cue the music and fade to black.

I know that the angels are real. I know that my conversations with God and His array of helpers are real.

I also know that experiences like the one above are enough to make any psychiatrist worth his salt consider putting me on medication.

But here's the thing: before this most recent encounter with the otherworldly, I felt pretty rotten. I feel better now. That aching, lingering malaise that had plagued me for so long has subsided. I'm getting things done now, I haven't lost my car keys in weeks, and I actually feel pretty good about myself. It's disconcerting to note that I am now having more memories of other sexual abuse experiences, things that make my skin crawl. But with each fresh memory, I call on my angels to help transmute and heal the energy. It isn't easy; God knows it's not easy. But I guess it's something that I must walk through right now.

Of course, I am not the only person in the world who has had this kind of experience. Many people are grasping at shadows, dealing with the same, vague suspicion that something sexually inappropriate occurred when they were children.

Memories may sneak into their sub-conscious minds, soak into dreams, or come slamming into their consciousness with ferocity. Other people I have met are certain that they were never molested, yet they still suffer from emotions related to sexual abuse.

The angels told me that all of us—whether we were actually sexually molested or not—are transmuting an energy as old as humanity itself. Some of us were, indeed, sexually abused in this current lifetime. Yet other people with these vague feelings may be suffering from memories of incidents that occurred in past lives, both as abuser and as victim. Some may be releasing a cellular memory of abuses that occurred to relatives in the past. Others are picking up on psychic pain that their neighbors, friends, and family members are enduring. And still others are processing energy that they absorbed when they were serving as a spirit guide or guardian angel to someone who was experiencing sexual abuse; the angel or spirit guide was so closely associated with the victim that they absorbed their charge's experience into their energy as if they themselves were experiencing it. Finally, there are some people that have simply agreed to experience this pain—despite never having been sexually abused—for the purpose of clearing the collective consciousness of horrific past abuses.

Why is all of this happening right now? The angels told me that humanity is undergoing an awakening, and a paradigm shift is occurring as a result of this awakening—the exploitation, sexual or otherwise, of any being for any purpose is unacceptable, plain and simple. In order to complete this shift, however, the pain of the collective consciousness of humanity must be transmuted, and that energy must be felt and finally cleared.

What is important to note here is that the angels say blame is not the purpose of this clearing work. Healing and releasing are the goals, not punishment. By all means, if a perpetrator is still alive, take the necessary steps to protect children from his or her proclivity and enact consequences, if appropriate. But the only thing that will truly relieve your pain is working through the emotions with the help of the angels, sitting in that agonizing space, and allowing the experience to carry you to a place of release and eventually, forgiveness.

If you are one of the millions around the world who are processing repressed memories of sexual abuse, healing the conscious memories, or working to heal the collective consciousness, the angels thank you. You are doing sacred work.

you want to know

whether i believe in ghosts

of course i do not believe in them

if you had known

as many of them as i have

you would not

believe in them either.

~Don Marquis

JILLIAN MILLER
NEW YORK, NY

J illian Miller, MS, MA, is a Ph.D. candidate in clinical psychology, an ANGEL THERAPY PRACTITIONER®, and a Theta Healing Practitioner™. She has been studying metaphysics for the past twenty years and has been a student of the Indian Spiritual Master Gurumayi Chidvilasananda since 1990, for whom she has also served on staff. Jillian lives in NYC with her husband and their three-year-old son, where she is dedicated to helping others align with their soul and with their Divine life path and purpose. As a new world teacher, she conducts workshops and healing circles, guiding others into deeper internal connections and greater cosmic awareness. She also offers one-on-one intuitive readings and healing sessions, both in person and over the phone.

Jillian has an extensive history working clinically with children, parents, and teachers, and has worked for many years as a developmental and mental health consultant in preschools and elementary schools throughout NYC. To contact Jillian, visit her website, www.DivineVibration.com, send her an e-mail at aligndivine@aol.com, or call her at (646) 438-0125.

Be Still and Know the Voice of God is Alive Within You: Remembrances of Grace and Divine Intervention

By Jillian Miller, MS, MA

It was just after the Christmas holidays, and I had been in a slump for several weeks. I knew at least part of the problem—I had stopped focusing on all that was good in my life and had begun to dwell on the things that weren't working. I had become frustrated by things my husband was doing and by things he wasn't doing. I was feeling bothered by the lack of time I had to myself. I was frustrated by my young son's sudden terror of sleeping in his room—both at night and during daytime naps—and the extended hours I was now spending to soothe him and help him settle into sleep. I was further agitated thinking of all the money, time, and energy I had spent to renovate our New

York City apartment and soundproof my son's new "big boy bedroom," only to discover that my husband and I had completely forgotten about the loud, clanging heating pipes that were now terrorizing our son and disrupting all of our sleep.

I could've gone on and on about all the things that were suddenly disturbing me and going awry in my life. I was working and running around so much that, without noticing, I had disconnected from the internal wellspring of ease, flow, abundance, grace, and love that had sustained me so bountifully for such an extended time.

What had happened? How had it happened? Up until that point, everything had seemed to be completely opening up for me. A sense of oneness and connection with all of life had begun to filter through my being. Joy, contentment, and enthusiasm were becoming more constant emotional states. Longstanding internal and external blocks and limitations seemed to be dissolving without effort. And wondrous, unexpected events and opportunities seemed to be manifesting at almost every turn. I was feeling aligned and on track with my life path and purpose, clear about where I was going, and infused with the fire to focus and take the steps to get there. Beyond what I had ever imagined, I could not help but notice that my life had become filled with magic.

However, suddenly I was lost. Where had it all so abruptly gone? My emotional state had begun spiraling downward, my vision was bleak, and I was struggling unsuccessfully to turn things around. Although I had sat for meditation repeatedly, seeking to reconnect, I was having great difficulty finding my way back. I longed to return to my inner core, to the state of deep connection and peace that nourished and soothed my entire being, infusing my world with inspiration, miracles, and meaning.

I had tried to disentangle from the weight of negativity that was pulling me down. I recognized there were great infusions of light beaming down onto our planet, affecting many of us as our bodies recalibrated to higher vibrational frequencies. I understood that, like many, I was undergoing a process of purification in which my lower personality traits were rising up and expressing themselves in the process of being expunged. Still, this understanding was not enough to shift me out of the psychic imprisonment in which I was dwelling.

I wanted to get back to my Source. I wanted to live connected and aligned. I was ready for my life to work. Yet, my own repeated efforts were leaving me dry. While I knew I needed to refocus on all the good and plenty that surrounded me, I could not seem to muster my will to do so in any adequate manner.

It was then, in a flash, that I remembered what I must do...*Call on the angels.* Without dwelling on the amnesia that had kept me from remembering what had elevated me out of countless similar seemingly immovable situations, I readied myself for the contact that I had neglected throughout this rough period. As I sat down in my meditation area, I prayed to the angels with a moment of urgency to *please release my resistance to perceiving all that is good and to expressing my gratitude.*

Following this prayer, I returned to my computer and came upon a message urging me to read an article about joy. As I read, my entire being became enlivened and alert. I was reminded that the emotions we all feel are nothing but energy; and while we may choose to label this energy in response to its variable intensity (e.g., depression, anger, anxiety, or fear), underneath these labels there is only Divine energy, whose essence is pure love, pure joy (Fenn, C., 2007). This was not the first time I was given this message, yet in this moment, my heart began stirring, sensing the truth in these words. If we could only remember to focus on the underlying energy, while recalling that it is God's joy-filled essence, we could circumvent and transmute many painful and turbulent internal experiences. And so, instead of becoming bound to the limiting energy embedded in a limiting emotional label, I was being reminded of an alternate option—I was free in each instant to choose: to dive beneath the label, to breath deep into the pulsations of energy throbbing within my body, and to remind myself that these are pulsations of God's energy and joy.

I didn't know exactly where this effort might lead, but I was ready to give it a go. As I tuned into my inner experience, I sensed a muckiness inside. In the past, I would have been quick to identify the sensations as negative—perhaps agitation, mixed with strands of despondency, anxiety, and/or apathy. However, on this night, I released my temptation to classify or probe my experience in this way. Instead, I allowed my entire consciousness to enter into the pulsations of energy. As I focused there I reminded myself, *This is God, this is God's energy, this is God's joy.*

With this simple act, blissful joy began to well up, right out of the very same space that I had initially sensed a throbbing of darkness and negativity. After weeks of sluggishness and disconnection, my entire body was suddenly bubbling with cheery, lively, sparkling pulses of life. As I delighted in these sensations, my heart and cells became fully alive, I was united with my heart, with the Divine heart, and with Divine bliss. Gratitude poured from me. There was nothing lacking, this was complete fulfillment.

Over the next several hours and days, there were recurrent moments when I found myself in the midst of intense energy that jolted me from my state of serenity. There were several occasions when I received shocking and disheartening news, there were times when I felt exhausted by fatigue, and there were occasions when another's words felt harsh or attacking. In each instant, as my awareness began to nose-dive into the web of ensnaring emotion, I stopped myself and concentrated instead on experiencing the throbbing energy deep within. As I again and again reminded myself that *this was God's energy and that these were pulsations of God's love,* my being, without fail, became saturated with sensations of pure joy and love. What could have been experienced as intensely painful affect was quickly and instantly transformed into a sublime and bliss-filled connection with my Source.

How incredibly simple this was. How powerfully and magically this elevated my perspective and my state. From worry, frustration, struggle, and gloom, I shifted instantly to rest in a place of complete unity, where everything was complete, where all was satisfactory, where all was in Divine order, where God's love and grace were ever-flowing. I felt complete protection, and I felt God and his celestial assistants with me, on my side, full of guidance, love, and support.

Each time I remembered to do this, one of the unexpected fruits that unfailingly followed was a spontaneous arising of gratitude. With it came the capacity to perceive, with clear knowing and trust, the unending current of grace and abundance that permeated my life.

The angels had heard and gratified my prayers with riches beyond anything I had ever conceived possible. How often the angels had blessed me similarly. In subtle ways, they had again and again elevated me into grace-filled territory.

And what I had learned from these celestial beings, time and again, was that I only needed to turn to them and ask for assistance. Once I did, they were awaiting eagerly to bestow heavenly blessings upon me. Yet they required my beckoning to do so. As I turned in their direction, my slightest step toward them was met with an all-embracing outpouring of love and generosity. With just the remembrance and calling of their name, they graciously began swinging open the most wondrous doors in both my inner and outer worlds, revealing infinite wells of joy, love, and bliss, and capabilities and possibilities—both mundane and sublime—that I never ever knew existed.

In time it became apparent that it was not only their sacred honor to serve me, but their holy mission to awaken and unite me with my own inherent greatness and Divinity, with the uninterrupted stream of ecstasy and delight that lay hidden within, and with my Divine life path and purpose. Yet it also became clear that they were available and eager to assist me in virtually any manner that would make my heart sing. As God's messengers, it is the angels' Divine duty to bring God's glory to the earth and to assist humanity in any way that will help to glorify God and to manifest God's will for peace and love across our planet (Virtue, D., 1999).

As I have witnessed many times over, there is truly no request that is too small or insignificant to bring to the angels. They can be in all places at once, they are not limited by our concepts of time and space, and they welcome the opportunity to assist in any way that will open our hearts to God's love. For, indeed, as we begin to smile and break down walls on the inside, we move another step closer to living as one with our Supreme Self. In such a state, we radiate God's love and light, our very presence brings blessings to the world, and each of our thoughts and actions helps to uplift our planet. This is the aim of the angelic realm.

For me, I had turned to the angels repeatedly, to assist me with a large range of issues and tasks. It has truly been my expanding relationship with these Divine beings that has accounted for a multitude of miraculous occurrences that have unfolded in my life. One of the most profound ways that they have helped me to transform my reality and draw forth different forms of abundance and expansion is by helping me relinquish internal blocks and resistance.

I noticed, for example, that even though I was wishing for some particular, desirable outcome, as the situation or thing began to draw near, I immediately erected invisible barriers to ward away those very things that I was working with great fervor to attract. There were clearly some internal conflicts that I was experiencing around allowing in the desires of my heart. Without further investigating what some of those conflicts may have been, however, I focused instead on beseeching the angels to *help me release my resistance to letting in the good.* That was all it took for my breath to expand and for some unseen internal wall to melt away. In this way, much good that I had been unable to let in throughout my life was suddenly beginning to enter. Even though I was unable to release internal opposition on my own, my angelic supporters never let me down. I came to see how my old blocks could instantly be dissolved simply by reaching out to those invisible heavenly helpers. It really was only a matter of my remembering to turn to them and ask.

In a similar vein, I also had a longstanding tendency to struggle and to find myself battling some overwhelming chaos or challenge. This stressful mode of being was familiar and habitual—and somewhat comforting. Yet it was also becoming increasingly undesirable and disruptive. Again, I merely had to remember that I was free to choose *ease*. By reaching out to the angels to help relinquish my resistance to ease, the still somewhat novel, yet exhilarating sensation of existing and operating in the flow became a more familiar and comfortable way of being.

Another big block I encountered, which kept Divine communion at bay, involved the judgments I held toward others and the unforgiveness that often followed. As I recognized this pattern, I turned to the angels once again to assist me in breaking free. On one particular occasion, I was experiencing great difficulty respecting and even tolerating the insights and communications being presented by another. It became evident that these judgments were precluding me from opening up to the supreme states of ecstasy and freedom that seemed to be within my reach. In a quiet moment, I came to see that my lack of tolerance for another was merely a reflection of the lack of tolerance I held for the same qualities within myself.

I then asked Archangel Raphael to help me release my judgments both toward this person and toward myself and to help me forgive us both for expressing ourselves in a manner that I was perceiving as *unrefined*. Upon seeing this person the next morning, I was thoroughly delighted and surprised to discover that I was reacting toward him with only warmth and acceptance. The angels had once again performed their magic, and some humbling had occurred within me. I felt a clearing, and the healing light of God illuminated my inner expanse.

There was another poignant occasion when my generally loving husband had an extremely negative reaction to something I said—which I had felt was completely innocent. As he expressed his anger, I began to struggle to maintain my own state of evenness and love. As anger and reactivity began to rise up from inside of me, I knew I did not want to relinquish the beautiful state I had worked so diligently to try to maintain. And so with great will I let go of my pride and called to Archangel Jophiel to *please beautify my thoughts*. In literally an instant, I was mysteriously able to gracefully express my understanding, validating my husband's point of view, then listen further to everything he wanted to say. Within a very brief period we had shifted back to a place of mutuality, partnership, love, and care.

There have been innumerable situations when the angels have come to my aid in more mundane ways and on more concrete levels. They have helped me almost daily to find parking spots and safeguard my car from parking tickets and vandalism. They have removed obstacles during my travels, manifested taxis, and assisted me with the return of a stolen purse and all its highly valued contents—from the man who had actually taken it. With each of these events, I felt touched by the angels' love, imbued with increased knowing that God is always there for me, wants the best for me, and that God and his angels love me and have never left my side.

In countless ways, the angels are waiting to enter our lives and help us to satisfy our greatest and smallest dreams and longings. All we need to do is seek their help—so why do we so often forget to turn to them and call? Although I have repeatedly become lost in the mire of worldliness, ensnared by my desires, attachments, and emotions, I have noticed that with each repeated effort I make toward connecting and co-creating with God's angelic team, the more imprinted and habitual this proclivity becomes. Then, I become more attuned to their frequent heavenly whispers and reminders.

When I asked my angelic guides if there was anything more they wanted to tell me on this topic, I heard the following:

> You are all creators of your reality. Why don't you stop and take a look around? Is this the life you have chosen to live? We are here to help you, work with you, to design the life of your dreams. Together, this world will turn into a paradise right before your eyes. Be still and know the voice of God is alive within you. Guidance and heavenly assistance is always at hand. It is time now to make a connection so we can assist you in all ways.

> As you ascend into the new world that is awakening now on your planet, it is time for you to listen to the voice of Heaven. It is time for you to awaken to the great truth of your being, the truth that you are one with your creator, who has never left your side. It is time to listen and then all great secrets will be revealed. It is time

for all to step up to the plate and assist in the process of transformation that the earth and her inhabitants are going through. It is time now to bring forth Heaven on earth...to glorify God and grant all your heart's desires, so that all can live in a state of love, blessing the earth and your brethren with each step you take...healing your hearts from fear, releasing the pain and heartaches you have carried for centuries. Break free and know you are God, we are one, all is grace.

Resources

Fenn, C. *A Conversation with Archangel Michael on Joy and Sorrow.* Starchild Ascension, 2006.

Virtue, D. *Healing with the Angels.* Hay House, 1999.

JULIE ZIMMERMAN
RALEIGH, NC

J ulie Zimmerman is an ANGEL THERAPY PRACTITIONER®, certified by Doreen Virtue, Ph.D. She is also a medium and Reiki Master. Julie is a dedicated healer and teacher who brings a practical approach to spiritual issues, helping her clients discover ways to use spirituality in everyday life. Her passion is assisting people to identify patterns in their lives, to tap into their own sense of inner wisdom, and to manifest their dreams into reality.

Julie is available for consultations, readings, and workshops. You can reach her at lightworker_julie@yahoo.com.

Rise Above It: The Art of Dealing with Difficult People

By Julie Zimmerman

We all have difficult people in our lives. None of us can escape this fact. From the noisy neighbor and the lazy co-worker to the overbearing boss and the talkative aunt, we all have people in our lives who try our patience and get on our nerves. Often we will go to great lengths to avoid these types of people—it seems so much easier to run away from them or wish them away than to deal with the problem at hand. Yet even as we try to get away, difficult people still seem to crop up.

It can feel like we are stuck at times, doomed to have the same types of people in our lives, dealing with the same issues over and over again. It can seem futile to make an effort or create change. However, I believe that if we learn to effectively deal with difficult people and understand why they are in our lives, we can minimize and potentially end the need to manifest such experiences. The more I discussed this topic with the angels and received their perspective about it, the more I learned and understood the gifts that difficult people provide, how we can recognize and honor the Divinity of difficult people, and ultimately, how to honor ourselves in the process.

The Gift of Difficult People

Believe it or not, difficult people are in our lives for a specific reason. It's not to make us suffer, to be mean to us, or to bring us down—although it may seem that way at the time. The angels say that difficult people provide some of the best and deepest opportunities to grow and learn, especially when they are family members. As we deal with difficult people, it can be helpful to remember this.

Difficult people bring us the gifts of awareness and attention. They show us that something within us is "off," that something needs to be healed or a lesson needs to be learned. It could be anything from healing a shadow aspect of ourselves or removing a deeply held belief to something more basic, such as learning patience and tolerance. Whatever it may be, this situation is more than likely necessary for our spiritual evolution. We may have been conscious of the need for healing in the past, but dealing with a difficult person will draw it to the forefront, into sharp relief. The good news is if you heal the vulnerable aspect of yourself and deal with the issue at hand, the need for the difficult person may no longer exist. He might even fade from your life or you may begin to interact with him in a more positive way.

Difficult people also bring us another gift: they remind us of our own safety and power. At one point, I wondered why it had to be so *difficult* dealing with difficult people. Why do things always turn into some kind of power struggle with them? Even a simple argument over replacing the batteries in a remote can turn into a battle of wills. The angels have shown me that the core issue here is fear—we are afraid they have the power to hurt us or control us. The reality is they don't. The only power they have is that which we give them. Archangel Michael says, *Do not fear, for they cannot harm you unless you let them. No one has that power over you. Stand in your own power lovingly and know that all is in Divine and perfect order.*

Honoring Difficult People

As you see the gifts that a particular difficult person brings to your life, you can see beyond the illusion and begin to see the underlying order within the situation. Perhaps as you do so, you can become more understanding of the difficult people in your life. You can honor them by focusing on the individuals behind the actions.

We are asked to remember that difficult people are *people*. They are no different than we are. They are merely trying their best, just like us, even if their best is not what it should be or, to be blunt, *sucks*. Often difficult people are acting out of their own pain, fear, and worries. The reality is we don't necessarily understand what people have been through or what has brought them to this point in life. We don't know what kind of day they had or what may have triggered them to cope in a non-effective way. However, they deserve a chance to learn and grow, just as much as we do.

Judging someone to be difficult is a subjective matter, anyhow. We tend to judge people, especially difficult ones, based on their weaknesses. And yet I've heard it said that our weaknesses are just our strengths with the volume turned up a little too loud. Let's say you have a talkative aunt, and you don't like being around her because you can't get a word in edgewise. To someone else, her chattiness could be energizing and fun. Another person might understand it as an eagerness to share. Your aunt might have friends, a husband, and kids who all love to be around her. This is the type of understanding and focus the angels are asking us to have.

Being understanding, however, does not mean you're excusing the behavior of difficult people. Their behavior at times can be quite inappropriate, even abusive. The point is we can be quick to judge difficult people and try to push against or resist them. It's easy for us to come to the conclusion that difficult people are somehow less deserving of help, guidance, and love. The angels have made it clear, however, that this isn't true. Difficult people may need love and compassion even more than we do.

We are all being given a call to compassion—a call to recognize and honor the Divinity of the difficult people in our lives. By remembering the oneness we share with others, we have a chance to break the pain reaction cycle that we have been involved in. We are asked to remember that worth and actions are separate things. This can be hard to accept in a world where worth is based almost completely on actions and what we do for others, but it is true, nonetheless.

One of the key tools that the angels brought to me to deal with the difficult people in my life is love. They taught me to surround the other person, the situation, and myself with love. Just focus on love. As it is said, *Only love is real.* By focusing on love, the illusion of conflict tends to fall away. It brings me back to that compassionate view of oneness. This approach has worked wonders for me and others.

For example, I had a client who was nervous about some high-maintenance relatives who were about to visit. He was concerned about how they would get along and how stressful their visit would be. The angels told him that instead of worrying, he should surround the entire situation with love in the days leading up to the visit. It really worked! He had a lovely visit with his relatives. Even his wife commented how pleasant the visit had been.

The angels say this is an important tool because, as stated above, there is a tendency to vilify difficult people. We lose sight of the fact that regardless of their behavior, difficult people are still Divine children of God. God asks us to love difficult people just as much as we would love ourselves or our children. God's love and compassion are unconditional—our love and compassion should be unconditional as well. By saying a person can't be some particular way or by saying a person needs to change, we are, in a way, making our love and compassion conditional. Loving a difficult person should be independent of his behavior. It is still our choice, however, to dislike the behavior and take steps to honor ourselves.

Honoring Yourself

Just as important as loving other people is loving and honoring yourself—respecting yourself and all that you are going through. It is so easy to negate your feelings during this process, to think you shouldn't feel a particular way or wonder if you're overreacting. Difficult people create strong and often painful emotional reactions in us, such as anger, fear, and sadness. Allow yourself to experience the feelings that arise without judging them or clamping down on them. Allow yourself the luxury of doing so, even if the feelings are uncomfortable. More than likely the feelings won't last. And although your feelings are part of the foundation of how you handle the situation, you don't necessarily have to act on them.

Clients frequently ask me, "Am I supposed to let this person walk all over me?" The consistent answer from the angels is, "No." This question is a reaction based on a fear that you are not safe. By honoring yourself, you are working towards creating and maintaining balance in the relationship. When dealing with difficult people, you are not asked to be a martyr, to love them grudgingly, or to sacrifice your truth. I know that in our society it's considered selfish or wrong to think of yourself, but it's perfectly valid to ask yourself how you feel about a particular situation and to consider what you need to feel safe and comfortable.

One of the ways you can honor yourself and strike a balance in relationships with difficult people is to set boundaries. Although there are numerous books on how to set boundaries, it remains a personal issue, rooted in your feelings, values, and goals. Only you can decide what is appropriate in your life. You have the right to place limits on what you are willing to experience in your life. Most of us have been raised with the belief that we can't say no, that we can't reject others' demands on our time and energy. I think this is mostly due to the fact that, in the past, boundaries have been approached from a win/lose standpoint. If we win and get what we want, then the difficult people we are dealing with lose. And often, boundaries are set out of anger and frustration. The angels say that boundaries are not meant to diminish the other person and need to be established from a place of love. Boundaries are meant to help us stand in the truth of who we are and what is right for us. Even if we need to be firm, we can do so from a loving place.

Often we refuse to set boundaries, afraid that we will hurt another's feelings. However, we suffer consequences when we refuse to set boundaries—anger, resentment, or even depression can set in. We also run the risk of overreacting at a later date, making a mountain out a molehill, so to speak. We can become so frustrated with another person that we can't be around him at all.

The angels want to make a few last points about setting boundaries and honoring ourselves. First, they ask us to be careful in choosing our battles. As stated earlier, even though we feel a particular way, we don't have to act on that feeling. We need to stop and ask ourselves: *How important is this issue? What can I live with? How important is this relationship to me?* If we are constantly finding fault with someone, there's probably another, deeper issue at hand. It can also be demoralizing for other people to be continually corrected. They might even find *us* difficult as a result and wind up setting boundaries to keep *us* in check.

Second, as much as a difficult situation might cause us strife and weigh on our minds, we have to let the issue go and move on. This will certainly need to be done on an emotional and spiritual level and possibly even a physical level if we decide we need to restrict contact with difficult people. Our goal in dealing with difficult people is not to change them or teach them a lesson. That is not our job. Our job is to change ourselves, through our thoughts, beliefs, and actions so that we manifest what we want. The Law of Attraction is very clear on this: whatever we focus on the most is what we get. By continually focusing on the negative part of the situation, we essentially hold difficult people in stasis and never allow them the chance to change.

How the Angels Can Help

Before closing, I would like to share some of the ways the angels can help us deal with difficult people. It can be hard to know what to do when we are in the midst of turmoil. The angels say it doesn't have to be difficult if we let them help.

The angels can show you why someone is in your life, what lesson there is to learn, or what pattern in your life needs healing. During a healing session, a friend of mine was given insight into why she had such a difficult time with an overbearing friend. She was shown that she still had unresolved issues with her parents and needed to learn more about standing up for herself in a loving way and claim her own power.

The angels can remind you to send love to the other person and show you in small ways that the difficult person is a *person*, just like you. One client of mine wasn't happy with his boss. He continually felt like his boss was just trying to make his life miserable. The angels showed him through some conversations with his boss that she felt just as overworked and stressed as he did. It gave him a sense of peace to know he wasn't the only one feeling these emotions.

The angels can also communicate with you through your thoughts and feelings, and tell you when it's time to honor yourself and set boundaries. You can ask for the angels' help in finding the right words so that you can express your truth in the best way possible, minimize any negative effects on the other person, and reach a harmonious agreement. You can also ask the angels to make you aware of any repetitive thoughts that are not attracting your highest good. They can help you shift these thoughts so that you focus on what you do want instead of what you don't want. As you change your thoughts, you should see changes occur in your life.

You can even call on specific angels to help with difficult people. There are several archangels who oversee relationships and can help with forgiveness, compassion, and love. Archangel Chamuel can bring you peace, Archangel Raguel can help with relationship harmony and fairness, Archangel Michael can protect you and help you stand in your own power, Archangel Gabriel can guide your words, and Archangel Jophiel can help you beautify your thoughts and focus on the positive. These are just a few of the angels who stand ready to help you at any time.

Summary

As you can see, the angels have given us a message of hope about dealing with difficult people, letting us know that these relationships are not meaningless or painful without a purpose. As you strive to resolve your issues that created the situation and balance the relationship, perhaps you can reach a point of mutual understanding and forgiveness. Maybe you can learn to let the difficult people in your life be who they are while you continue to be who you are.

We have such a unique opportunity at this point in our lives and evolution. We have the opportunity to see beyond the veil, to see the gift within even the most difficult of circumstances, to recognize our oneness with the Universe, and to see the Divinity within everything, including ourselves. We are truly the creators of our experience, and we can change it as we see fit.

I know as I go forward in my life I will be looking at difficult people differently. Hopefully I will approach them in a more loving and effective manner. I will be asking myself some different questions as part of the process: What issue is this situation bringing up for me? How can I use this information to heal myself and spiritually evolve? How can I approach these people with love and respect for their Divinity? How can I honor myself and better define who I am and what is appropriate for me?

My prayer is that you find beauty, love, and joy in all that is around you. I pray that you know that you are safe and loved no matter what, and know that the angels are ready to help you, even during the most difficult of situations. All you need to do is call.

Resources

Virtue, D. *Archangels and Ascended Masters: A Guide to Working and Healing with Divinities and Deities.* Hay House, 2003.

Virtue, D. *Archangel Oracle Cards.* Hay House, 2004.

DR. PANNEY WEI
LOS ANGELES, CA

Panney Wei is an award-winning artist whose heritage is deeply rooted in Chinese history as a proud descendant of China's greatest military hero, General Tso Tsung-Tang, forever immortalized by his famous cuisine, General Tso's Chicken. With her background in alternative medicine, gained from surviving a near-death experience with the life-threatening illness, bulimia, Panney has first-rate knowledge about the power of the mind-body connection, living life with purpose, and the ability to achieve anything in life. She healed herself without the help of doctors and later became a doctor of naturopathy and a certified practitioner of several powerful healing modalities, including hypnotherapy, neuro-linguistic programming, life coaching, and Reiki. She maintains a thriving practice empowering women, children, and entrepreneurs with successful strategies to achieve their dreams and live their happiest, most fulfilling lives! Nationally recognized as a Presidential Scholar for exceptional talent in the arts, Panney began her entertainment career as a professional figure skater, but parlayed her talents into TV and radio hosting, speaking, and writing, where her true passions shine.

Recognized as "The Asian American Entertainer to Look Out For" by APEX, she has hosted for *NBA TV*, *The Money Show*, and *Discovery Channel*, and hosts her live weekly radio show focused on personal growth and empowerment, *Positive Changes with Panney Wei*, broadcast in over 220 countries. As a writer, Panney's interviews and articles have been featured internationally in leading publications including *The LA Times*, *China Gate*, *China Daily News*, and *Woman International Magazine*. She is currently working on her upcoming memoir about personal heroism and survival of the human spirit, *The Jade Princess Warrior*. Her website is www.panneywei.com.

The Jade Princess Warrior

By Dr. Panney Wei, N.D., C.Ht.

I have a memory of being in the womb and of not wanting to be born. I knew somehow, intuitively, that life would not be easy and that I had to be ready for what was to come. If life was a series of lessons and incarnations, then I was an old soul that decided to come back one last time, just for the heck of it, and make this life as hard as I could so that I could learn all my lessons and never come back. But not just yet.

—Excerpt from Panney's upcoming memoir,
The Jade Princess Warrior

When I was a little girl, I knew I was destined for something meaningful and something profound in this lifetime, and that my life would have a sacred purpose. I didn't know what that was at the time, but I knew I was going to achieve something powerful, and I was meant to give it back to the world. I could feel it in my heart and in my bones. It was an inner knowing, deep inside, that sometimes life would be challenging, but I would have guidance from God and my angels to light my way, and the lessons I learned from this lifetime would be my legacy for my children, my fellow man, and for the world.

Little did I know that the gift I would give back to the world would be my first memoir, *The Jade Princess Warrior*. It's about personal heroism, overcoming extraordinary obstacles, and survival of the human spirit, fusing the mystery and richness of the East with the West. It is an inspiring account of my coming of age, and of how I overcame dominating social issues that young women face, like poor self-esteem, body image, falling in love, fitting in, pleasing your parents, and finding your bliss. It is also an entertaining mother-daughter story about my relationship with my mother, who projected all of her frustrations on me as a result of the trials and tribulations of her loveless, arranged marriage, and how that colored my life. It is a universal story about our mutual search for identity, self-worth, and love, but more importantly, it's about my coming home to Who I Am.

Since I was a child, angels were always a part of my life. When we first immigrated to America at age two, my parents placed me in the best school on the block. It was a Catholic school and gave me my first exposure to angels and saints, who were considered special guides in Catholicism. Since education is so important to Chinese culture, my parents weren't concerned that these two types of luminaries were promoted in the school; they just wanted me to have the best education possible.

Blissfully, I spent much of my youth drawing and painting pictures of angels and scenes from nature. They were a source of comfort in my life. But when I was five, we moved to California. Once again, I was placed in the best school in the area; this time, a Baptist Christian school. However, because the school was so conservative, my exposure to angels was suddenly cut short from my awareness, and it wasn't until I was in my early twenties, when I survived a near-death experience after my five-year battle with bulimia, that angels miraculously reappeared in my life.

The bulimia was first triggered when I was a young teenager facing the overwhelming pressures of my highly competitive environment and struggling with being perfect, staying thin, and being a champion figure skater. I was adjusting to American life, balancing it with the values of my Asian-American heritage of saving face, of silence, of service, and of duty to family before oneself. In my childhood, I was a high achiever—a champion figure skater by the age of eleven. Ice skating was my passion, my greatest joy, and my escape from the demands of life. When I was skating, I felt like I was contributing to the world through my talents, my vision, my artistry, and my soul. I felt I had a purpose, and because of that, my life had meaning. At a very young age, I was blessed with understanding the feeling of living your life with purpose and bliss that opens the doors to abundance in so many forms.

But my mother, because of circumstances that led her to feel uncertain of her position in life and her marriage, lived through me vicariously. She pressured me to perform, win, be perfect, and to give her everything I possessed to fulfill her unfulfilled dreams; I basically lost myself in the process and nearly lost the joy of performing. At a very young age, I learned what it was like to sacrifice oneself for another's happiness. I felt trapped and alone. Daily I would hear taunts such as, "You're too fat," "Don't be stupid," "If you're not perfect, you're not going to win." But somehow, I didn't let all the negative reinforcement bring me down or affect my performance. In fact, I had a mean winning streak for years, winning first in each and every competition. When I was skating, my spirit was soaring, my heart was full of joy, and I was happy. It gave me a sense of purpose and fulfillment in my heart, and is what I know now as an adult as *living your life with purpose*, and living your life on the *highest vibration* possible that matches your soul's truest expression.

But there's a twist in my story: because of financial stress and pressure from family members, my parents decided to clip my wings. They pulled me off the ice in the blink of an eye, without my consent, shattering my Olympic dreams faster than I could finish my triple salchow. One day I was ice skating. The next day I wasn't. Skating was like breathing to me. When it was taken away from me, I was devastated. What would I do now? Reinvent myself? Yes, I had no choice. Somehow, I had to cope. In Chinese culture, we respect and revere our elders, and therefore, I believed they knew what was best for me. I was only fifteen years old. If I didn't listen to my parents, what would happen to me? As a teenager, I felt voiceless, helpless, and inadequate, all ingredients that create a modern-day bulimic; in my little head, the downfall of my skating career was due to my not being good enough as a figure skater, not good enough for my family, not good enough for my career. Nobody told me otherwise.

This sent me into a deep depression that I battled daily with my natural sense of humor, faith, and never-ending optimism. But bulimia had already planted its ugly seed within me and was breeding a life of its own. It felt like a slow suicide. Throughout high school, where I graduated with honors, I was a class officer, varsity athlete, and cheerleader, and throughout college, where I was still a highly functioning young adult, bulimia became a monster that controlled my life. To the world, I looked like the perfect person and student, but in reality, my world was crashing beneath me. My eating disorder was not so much about how I felt about my body, but how I felt about myself. I missed my days as an ice skater, which always brought me breathless joy as a human being. But now, all I could feel was a sense of loss, of being voiceless and misguided, like something was missing in my life. Where were my angels? Unbeknownst to me, they were always by my side, but angels are governed by a very simple law, the Law of Free Will, and they cannot interfere in our lives unless we ask them to. We have the free choice to live our lives as we wish, and angels can only intervene when they are asked. The only exception is if there is a life-threatening situation, as in my case, they will come to the rescue without delay.

I had heard about girls throwing up in the high school bathroom, in the gym, and especially at the ice skating rink before competitions, and I innocently fell into this prevalent social disease and epidemic that affects so many young women in this country and abroad. The U.S. has the highest percentage of young adults suffering from bulimia, claiming 5 million lives per year. Bulimia became a way for me to control the pressure and stress in my life, to control *something* when everything else seemed out of control, and to find solace in myself. I catapulted into a downward spiral of binge eating and purging, and fell into inappropriate methods of weight control, experimenting with diet pills, laxatives, and liquid diets. I ate to try to fill a hunger and a void. But once I was full, the emptiness was still there. I was searching to feed my soul what it had lost: its purpose in life; its will to live.

The binging and purging became an obsession, in body, mind, and soul. Eventually, even if my body wanted to stop, my mind just couldn't. There was a disconnect. Where once I thought I had control over the disease, now the disease controlled me. Bulimia had ruined my body, throwing my metabolism and physiology into disarray. My electrolytes were completely unbalanced, to the point of causing possible heart disease, and I was spinning out of control.

One day, in the middle of my purging, alone in a locked bathroom, my heart stopped for a second, and I ran out of breath and passed out. In this small but significant moment of darkness, when nobody was around, I had a powerful near-death experience that changed my life forever. I learned that only I was responsible for my life. Not God. Not the angels. It was only me. Every bit of it...me. I created my reality, whether it was good or bad—even my reality after death. And in this instant of darkness, with nobody around, my soul went somewhere quiet, black, depressing, and lifeless. I caught a glimpse of what my life would be if I continued down this path. It was like a scene out of the movie *What Dreams May Come,* when the wife of Robin William's character commits suicide, and her soul goes to her own version of hell, a purgatory that she created and was trapped within. I stayed in this very dark and dismal space for just a moment, and when I snapped out of this experience, I knew I had to change my direction in life. I had to choose to LIVE, to get back my life, to rediscover who I was. I had to take steps to ensure my health and happiness again, and to heal myself from this illness. It was then that my life and life's purpose were back on track.

In the following days and years of my recovery, it was as if angel wings carried me, giving me strength, protection, and comfort. I remembered my childhood when I first learned about angels and instantly believed they were with me. They had intervened because my illness was life threatening and I hadn't yet fulfilled my destiny on earth. Thank goodness! I was at eighty pounds for my petite 5'4" frame and so weak from bulimia that I could barely walk. My hair was falling out; my face was swollen from purging. But even though my body was weak, my spirit was strong. Somehow, I found my strength, my inner calling, to make something of my life again. Making the decision to LIVE started me on the powerful journey back to true abundance, happiness, and health.

I decided to take matters into my own hands. Western forms of medicine were not an option for me. Bulimia was a relatively new disease at the time, and my parents didn't know quite how to cope, so I had to fight this battle alone. I made a clear-cut decision that I would save myself from this disease using alternative medicine, without the help of doctors, armed only with my faith in God, myself, and the power of my mind. Each and every time I prayed or meditated, I would call on God and the four major archangels—Raphael, Michael, Gabriel, and Uriel—to protect me and guide me to the right people or resources that would help me.

To heal myself, I immersed myself in books about changing my physiology, and my mental and emotional chemistry, and I embarked on the journey to self-healing, using wisdom acquired through countless hours of study in natural and alternative medicine, meditation, philosophy, Reiki energy healing, and psychology. Anything that would beat this disease. I became a Merlin, a shape-shifter, a Jade Princess Warrior, to slay this disease, this terrible dragon, and finally put it to rest.

I discovered a secret: the mind is supremely powerful, so powerful that when you take your mind somewhere, whether to a fantasy or an image of something you desire—especially a vision of healing and abundance—the body will certainly follow. Olympic athletes do it, multi-million-dollar businessmen do it, I did it. It works.

The journey towards healing myself and my relationship with my mother, who was my first glimpse of the goddess in my life, became a spiritual quest for me that brought me full circle to where I am now. From this extraordinary experience, my belief that I could self-heal and achieve anything I desired in life, even rise above physical limitations, was fully cemented, and this ugly dragon, bulimia nervosa, was overcome.

How did I accomplish this? With the guidance of God, the power of my mind, and the medicine of optimism, self-awareness, hope, and humor, not to mention a dash of forgiveness and compassion, and a pinch of sass to keep things interesting. Writing about my experiences, my relationship with my mother, and how I healed myself, as well as finally discovering real love in my life with my husband and manifesting true abundance, has now become my gift to the world.

Bulimia became my biggest lesson, my biggest enemy, and my biggest gift in self-love and recognizing my inner power. It is the reason I now dedicate my life to empowering others, leading by example and continuing the journey to heal myself. Now I am finally fulfilling my life's purpose to entertain, empower, and inspire people to live more forceful lives, to bring comfort and transformation to them through my writing, teaching, and motivational speaking, and to take those steps in sharing my knowledge to help heal nature, the world, and its precious human beings, from the inside out, one amazing person at a time.

I can now be my own person with everything I've overcome, be the person I was meant to be, and experience my achievements as my own, without anyone holding me back. This is what I would love to inspire young people and women to achieve for themselves. It is my desire to prevent them from tumbling down the same road I did. I want to let them know that they're loved and not alone. I want to prevent them from wasting precious time spent binging and purging in the bathroom in secrecy, from hiding from who they really are, when they could be out in the world, falling in love, achieving their dreams, and living their beautiful and rich lives.

Every woman and man has the ability to change the world, to live a life with purpose, to harness inner power, and clearly follow the murmurs of the heart. Everyone can be the star of his or her life and turn every challenge into a victory. That's what I call *"living in abundance."* Nobody is born by accident. Everyone has a special purpose to fulfill in this world that only he or she can accomplish.

But it's up to you to have the courage to go and find it. It can be fun! Ask God and your angels to help you as they helped me. Only then will you know how deeply loved you are. Only then will you know that you're never alone.

When you live your life on purpose, and not unconsciously or at the mercy of others, a world of opportunities opens for you that you could never have dreamed possible, and your life is transformed instantly. This is what God, the angels, and the Universe desire for you. Believe it. Dream it. Everybody deserves the amazing life they were meant to live, and it is my hope and belief that you will find yours, too.

Only by healing the Universe within yourself and your body are you then able to heal the Universe outside yourself, and eventually, the world. The writing of my memoir and my profound experiences in overcoming my illness and struggles as a young Asian-American woman have been the start of that journey for me. Now I write to heal my heart, to change the world, to connect with you—to empower others and give a voice to the voiceless so that you know you're not alone.

Thorns and stings

And those such things

Just make stronger

Our angel wings.

~Emme Woodhull-Bäche

SUSAN DINTINO
NEW YORK / FLORIDA

Susan Dintino is a graduate of SUNY Buffalo and author of the children's book, *A Year of Me*. She also writes magazine articles, poetry, and is currently working on her next books, *Lessons I Learned on the Way to 60* and *Daily Affirmations for a Well-Lived Life*.

Susan is an ANGEL THERAPY PRACTITIONER®, certified by Doreen Virtue, Ph.D. She is also a trained medium and a professional spiritual teacher. Her other certifications include Reiki Master and Reconnective Healing Practitioner Level III®. Susan's work is her passion, and her business, Wishes & Dreams LLC, promotes her books, private readings, healing work, workshops, and weekend seminars.

With her husband, Dennis, Susan has dual residences in Williamsville, New York, and Sanibel Island, Florida. Her three daughters, two sons-in-law, and two grandchildren are all treasured and reinforce her belief that nothing is more important than to love and be loved in return. To learn more about Susan, visit her website at www.susandintino.com, or email her at wish2be@aol.com.

Like Yourself...
Love Yourself... Today!

By Susan Dintino

I thought long and hard about what my contribution to this anthology should be. The angels have touched me in numerous ways, and deciding which experience to put to print was a daunting task. Should I write about the angel feathers or pins I have found when I was feeling desperate and looking for guidance and answers? Or should I relate the experience I had when, after all else failed, the angels paved a way for me to gain access to a workshop that was totally sold out? The more I thought, the more confused I became until I realized that I should consult my friends, the angels, for the answer.

Quietly entering meditation, I asked for their guidance; as usual, this loving realm did not disappoint me. They gently reminded me of the book I am writing entitled *Lessons I Learned on the Way to 50.* This book has become such an exercise in procrastination that I recently changed the title to *Lessons I Learned on the Way to 60*! They told me that the first chapter of this book is the most important lesson I have learned, and thus, it's the one I most need to share with you. Proudly, with angelic blessings, I present you with this selection.

Like Yourself...Love Yourself...Today!

"To love is first of all to accept yourself exactly as you are."
—*Thich Nhat Hanh*

I have been dieting ever since I can remember. I have kept journals and diaries all my life, and I have a recorded date of my first diet; it was in the sixth grade. It is sad, but true. I have been up and down the scale so many times that I think I have lost and regained a small African country. I had clothes in my closet that could fit my six-year-old granddaughter and clothes that could house that small African country. I was the greatest dieter in the world. I have measured the ounces of my food on a tiny scale. I have eaten eggs, eggs, and more eggs on a diet that I was assured the U.S. Ski Team used. I have made soups that eat your fat away and have drunk drinks that gave me more pep than I knew what to do with.

All to no avail. I lost weight, oh yes, I lost it, but I soon regained it all plus a few pounds more for good measure. Sadly, I became a statistic—one of the thousands of people that lose weight only to gain it back. The comforting fact, if you can call it that, is that I am in the majority. Now, if that is the case, being the intelligent person that I am, I had to ask myself, *Why am I dieting if these diets don't work? Why are any of us doing this? Why are so many of us are caught in this trap? How much time in my life has been wasted counting calories, protein grams, and carbohydrates?*

As I took a closer look at these questions, I could feel my guardian angels gently nudging me, telling me that it was time to stop a cycle that was clearly not working.

They guided me to take a closer look at the reasons why I engaged in these dietary acrobatics. I was pretty sure I was not a closet masochist addicted to self denial, so why would I put myself through all this? I felt if I could answer this question, it would bring me one step closer to understanding the root of my problem. It dawned on me that my incentive for dieting was pure and simple: every time I looked in the mirror, a fat woman looked back at me. Regardless of what I weighed, I always saw that same fat woman's reflection. With extreme displeasure, I would yell at her, demean her, and say things to her I would never say to my worst enemy. Looking at pictures of myself taken throughout the years, I realized that I never was as fat as I saw myself. It was just my perception of that woman in the mirror—a woman I just did not like very much, let alone love. I realized that changing my body was not the answer. I had done that and I still wasn't happy with myself. The time had come for me to go deeper and change myself from the inside, to find the elusive me who could be happy just the way I was in the present moment. No conditions. No self judgments. Just acceptance.

My first step was to stop the verbal abuse I heaped on myself whenever I looked in the mirror. I realized that by telling myself on a daily basis how obese I was, I was actually creating a self-fulfilling prophecy. The more I criticized myself, the worse I felt, and the worse I felt, the more I ate. There was nothing as soothing as a two-pound bag of Jelly Bellies to bring me comfort. The problem was that this comfort brought along with it the extra pounds, and before I knew it, poof! I had manifested that fat woman in the mirror. I decided I had to look at myself in a new light. I had to break the old negative reflection I saw and replace it with a new positive image. I had to have a plan. I had to approach my reflection with a new set of eyes. I had to try to see myself with the same unconditional love and acceptance that my angels did.

Slowly and cautiously, I approached the mirror, preparing myself for my new attitude. When I looked at my reflection, I forced myself to remain neutral and say a brief prayer of gratitude. If any critical thoughts came to mind, I would "cancel and delete" the thought and look away from the mirror.

My next step was to make a list of my positive attributes and form them into complimentary affirmations. Armed with a flattering remark, I approached the mirror and said to my reflection, "You have beautiful eyes." And then I said a prayer of gratitude. It is important to note here that I allowed myself the feelings of accepting the compliment. I would not only say the words, but I would feel the emotion that went along with them. I would smile at myself as I made eye contact and say "I like you just the way you are now." In order to change—really change—I knew I had to alter the way I *felt* about myself, not just the way I talked to myself.

At first, complimenting myself felt unnatural and even silly, but believe me, it worked. It transformed the way I felt about myself and ultimately, the way I saw myself. The more I performed this exercise, the easier and more successful it became.

One of the benefits of seeing myself in a positive light is that it was easier for me to accept compliments from others. I was the type of person who had a real problem graciously accepting praise. I always distrusted the motive. *Are they just being kind? What do they want now? They can't possibly mean I look great. Do their glasses need an adjustment? If only they knew what I weigh, they would take that compliment right back.*

I never felt I deserved a compliment that pertained to my appearance, or anything else, for that matter. In no way did I believe it was truthful. One of the bonuses of my mirror exercise was the realization that I could accept a compliment without rationalizing it away. I deserved it. Now, when someone compliments me, I am able to smile, say "thank you," and be proud of the woman I am.

The next step for me in this Divinely guided acceptance process was to look at myself totally nude and not become violently ill. I am a pretty free spirit where nudity is concerned and have been known to walk around the house *sans* clothing. However, no one was ever around in those times to see me, nor did I allow myself to ever really look in the mirror. I was a closet nudist. Now it was as if the angels were saying that if I was going to really accept myself, I had to go all the way. This was no time for cowardice.

So one morning, before my shower, I stood totally naked in front of the mirror and did the unthinkable. I looked at myself. Not just a furtive glance. I really looked. At first, I was horrified.

I quickly looked away and jumped into the shower, hoping that this sight would not give me post-traumatic stress syndrome. As the warm water of the shower relaxed me, the angels reminded me that the whole point of this exercise was to show myself kindness, to treat myself the way I would a dear friend. I soaped up and decided to approach my body with an attitude of gratitude. "How fortunate I am to have a healthy body," I told myself. "This body has served me well. It has always been there when I needed it, and although I am sure there are times I have let it down, it has never let me down. This body, just as it is right now, right this minute, is a blessing. Thank you, God."

When I got out of the shower, I took another look at myself. It amazed me how my perception had changed. I noticed my belly and the stretch marks there, and fondly remembered the three babies who lived there for a time. The breasts that once stood proud now drooped, but I remembered those same babies feeding there and the tenderness of their mouths. Yes, this body with all of its so-called flaws has served me well, and with this realization came the first stirrings of acceptance. I now look at my body every day with blessings and gratitude and know it reflects the kind, loving woman I am.

Pictures of me were the last stumbling block I had to overcome. I was the only one in the house without a portrait of myself prominently displayed. My daughters teased me that if I ever disappeared and they needed a recent photograph, the only one they had was the one on my driver's license. That picture could only be compared to a mug shot of someone who had lost a week's sleep and was having a very, very bad hair day.

It was enough to get me motivated to have a new portrait made. The problem was I hated having my picture taken. I could never stand the way I looked in the finished photos, and I was a master at avoiding the camera. The tactics I used were various and masterful. Unselfishly, I would volunteer to take the picture, holding the camera with the authority of Annie Leibovitz; or in a panic, I would dash off right before the bulb flashed with the excuse of a weak bladder. If all my subterfuge failed, I would position myself in the picture in such a way that you would be lucky to see me at all. I usually looked like a floating head with a toothy smile. The Cheshire cat had nothing on me. Everyone would look at the picture and ask where I was. They would usually need a magnifying glass to find me. I decided that on my road to self-acceptance, this behavior would have to stop.

For Christmas that year, I decided I would take the plunge and have my picture taken professionally. After the license picture comment, I felt this would be a great surprise gift for my family. Planning every detail, I began my photo day with a pampering session at the hair salon. I wanted to feel special from the top of my head to the tips of my toes. I had carefully selected a few outfits, not focusing on what did or did not make me look fat, but instead on colors I loved and clothing that made me feel good about myself.

As the pictures were being taken, I encouraged myself to go with it and play the super model for a few hours. I loved it! When the proofs arrived, I excitedly tore open the envelope and my face fell as I looked at them. I detested them all and felt like I looked FAT! Fortunately, the angels were there to stop a potential downward spiral. They redirected my energy and reminded me that I was using an old perception of myself and judging myself in a negative way. I would not be stopped. I selected the picture I thought was the best, and the more I looked at it and focused on my positive attributes, the more I liked what I saw. Carefully, I selected frames for each of my family members, and on Christmas Day, I presented my portrait to them with pride. They "oohed" and "ahhed" and loved them. In each of their homes, I took a place of honor, and every time I look at the 8 x 10-inch photo on the mantle of our fireplace, I am proud of the woman I see there. Since then, I frequently have pictures taken with family and friends. There are times I look marvelous and times that I don't. The difference is now I can look at the photographs with a sense of humor, focusing on the occasions they were taken and the wonderful memories that they hold.

The angels taught me my first lesson on the road to sixty: I am not numbers on a scale or a diet failure statistic. I am not a jeans' size or a chronological age. My value is in the beauty I see in myself each time I look in the mirror and appreciate the woman standing there. The confidence I now possess has taken me on a path of self discovery and awareness that I would not have thought possible. As I released the burdens of self-judgment, I became less judgmental of others. As I became loving and more compassionate towards myself, I became more loving and more compassionate towards others. With this change came my profound realization. It is only by accepting and truly loving ourselves just the way we are, right at this moment, that we can truly accept and love one another.

Just the Beginning

The angels knocked upon his door
And said,
"Your suffering's done.
It's time for you to fly away
And dance upon the sun.
Our wings will enfold you
With the deepest love
We will escort you
To the light
And God above."
Our dear one smiled
And his soul took flight
A shooting start across the sky
In the darkest night.

~ Susan Dintino

CATHERINE MCMAHON
COUNTY WICKLOW,
IRELAND

Catherine McMahon has been communicating with angels and ascended masters all her life. From her early childhood, she remembers holding conversations with Jesus and her guardian angels.

Catherine is an ANGEL THERAPY PRACTITIONER®, certified by Dr. Doreen Virtue, Ph.D. She has a thriving healing practice, conducting angel readings and preforming energy work. She travels around Ireland teaching Angel Guidance Practitioner certification courses. She also teaches the Usui method of Reiki in venues around County Wicklow, Ireland, where she lives.

You may contact Catherine for a reading, treatment, or to learn details about her courses by visiting her website, www.DivinePrescriptions.com, or emailing DivinePrescriptions@gmail.com.

Opening the Pathways of Angelic Communication

By Catherine McMahon

When I teach classes about angels, the most common question I am asked is, "How do we receive Divine guidance, and how can we open these gates of communication?"

I have found that those students who have clear, bright chakras—energy vortexes within the body—tend to have more success in further developing their psychic channels. Therefore I want to talk about the different channels of communication we use to receive messages from the Divine and the chakras associated with them.

The Four Channels of Divine Communication

We all have four channels that allow us to receive Divine communication, known as the "four clairs." Whenever we receive Divine messages, we do so through our clairs. No channel is more effective or less effective than the other—they are simply different vehicles of communication.

Clairvoyance, or "clear seeing," is the channel used when we see things with the mind's eye, either outside the body or inside the mind. You may see symbols, mental movies, or photo-like pictures, or you may see angels, deceased loved ones, or animals. Some people have the ability to see these things with their eyes open, in an opaque fashion, while others simply see them in their "imagination," or mind's eye—with their eyes either open or closed.

Seeing colors, auras, angel lights, or visions from the corner of your eye are also examples of clairvoyance. Angel lights are either colored or white lights that trail across our vision. White lights are your guardian angels, and colored lights are archangels. These lights are the reflection of their aura.

The chakra involved in clairvoyant experiences is the third eye chakra, located between and slightly above the eyebrows.

Clairaudience, or "clear hearing," is identified when you hear a voice, either outside of yourself or inside you head. The voice might sound like someone else's or like your own. You may also hear a song over and over again in your head—take note of the lyrics in the song and you will probably find a message that will be of assistance.

Some people often hear a high-pitched noise in their ear, sometimes mistaken for tinnitus, or "ringing in the ear." This is the way angels download information to us. If it is too bothersome, you can ask them to lower the volume.

Also, some people have reported hearing a choir of angels during times when they needed additional guidance or support.

Other noises sometimes heard include bells or whistles, or the sound of someone calling your name repeatedly. If this happens, just pause and acknowledge that a heavenly helper is trying to get your attention. Clear your mind and see if you can hear an additional message from your angels!

Clairaudience is linked with the ear chakras.

Clairsentience, or "clear feeling," is identified when the person receiving the messages is doing so through physical or emotional feelings within the body. Clairsentience may be experienced by feeling hot or cold sensations, a tense feeling in your gut, an emotional feeling that something isn't quite right, or a peaceful feeling that indicates that everything is going to be fine.

Picking up on someone else's physical ailment or pain, or feeling someone's emotions as if they were you own are also examples of clairsentience.

Also, feeling someone brush past you when there is no one there, feeling someone brush your cheek, or gently tugging your hair are examples of clairsentience.

Smelling a particular scent that seems to come from no discernable source is also clairsentience. Odors like apple pie, lilies, roses, or a heavenly indescribable scent may remind one of a deceased loved one and may be the loved one's way of communicating that they're safe and happy. This type of clairsentience is actually a sub-category, called clairalience, meaning "clear smelling."

Clairsentience is governed by the heart chakra.

Claircognizance, or "clear knowing," is knowing that something is going to happen without being told or suddenly having complete knowledge about something without having any prior knowledge of it. Claircognizants know how to fix broken objects without having to look at the instructions, despite being unfamiliar with the item's construction. People who are claircognizant may also receive ideas and inspiration that will save them time and money, seemingly out of the blue. Knowing the course a relationship or business venture will take from the onset is also a type of claircognizance. When asked how they know a piece of information, you will often hear a claircognizant person say, "I just know."

This type of Divine communication is related to the crown chakra.

The Chakra System

The chakra system refers to the energy systems within our subtle bodies. The word chakra is Sanskrit for "wheel." This is how a chakra is perceived—as a whirling vortex of energy. There are seven major and twenty-one minor chakras in the body. Chakras work as energy transformers, accessing Universal energy and stepping it down to a lower frequency to use in the physical body. The chakra system transmits energy between layers of a person's aura, the energy field within and surrounding the body. This energy then directs the hormonal and physiological systems within the physical body, affecting the physical body.

The chakra system location corresponds with the major nerve plexuses on the physical body. The major chakras are situated in a vertical line ascending from base of the spine to the crown of the head. Each chakra on the front of the body is paired with its counterpart on the back, with the exception of the base and crown chakras, which point downward toward the earth and upward toward Heaven, respectively. The front aspect of the other major chakras relates to the person's feelings, the back relates to the person's will.

The following is a brief description of each chakra:

THE ROOT, OR BASE, CHAKRA—FIRST CHAKRA

The root, or base, chakra is the first chakra. It is situated at the base of the spine near the coccyx bone. It vibrates the color red. Its main issue is that of survival and physical needs. It is associated with the adrenal gland and the reproductive and skeletal systems.

- Imbalances in this chakra lead to lethargy, difficulty in achieving inner quiet, and osteoarthritis.
- Aromatherapy essential oils that are associated with the base chakra are cedarwood, myrrh, and patchouli.
- Associated crystals include bloodstone, tiger's eye, and hematite.
- The musical note associated with this chakra is G.

- Archangel Gabriel is the angel associated with the root chakra.

THE SACRAL CHAKRA—SECOND CHAKRA

The sacral chakra, sometimes referred to as the hara, or sexual chakra, is the second chakra. It is situated just below the umbilicus. It vibrates the color orange, and its main issues include sexuality, forgiveness, and emotional balance. It is associated with the sex organs and the bladder.

- Imbalances in this chakra lead to bladder and prostate problems, impotence, frigidity, lower back pain, emotional instability, and feelings of isolation.
- Aromatherapy essential oils related to the sacral chakra include rose, jasmine, and sandalwood.
- Crystals include golden topaz, citrine, and carnelian.
- The musical note associated with this chakra is A.
- Archangel Zadkiel is the angel associated with the sacral chakra.

THE SOLAR PLEXUS—THIRD CHAKRA

The solar plexus is the third chakra, and is situated in the upper abdomen, below the lower tip of the sternum. It vibrates the color yellow, and its main issue is centered around self-power and will. It is associated with the pancreas, and the muscular and digestive systems.

- Imbalances in this chakra lead to ulcers, digestive problems, allergies, diabetes, control issues, low self-esteem, and an over-sensitivity to criticism.
- Associated essential oils are those of vertivert, ylang ylang, and bergamot.
- Associated crystals include aventurine, quartz, sunstone, and yellow citrine.
- The musical note associated with this chakra is B flat.
- Archangel Uriel is the angel associated with the solar plexus chakra.

THE HEART CHAKRA—FOURTH CHAKRA

The heart chakra is the fourth chakra, and it is situated in the mid-sternal region, directly over the heart and the thymus gland. It vibrates the color green, and its main issues are love and relationships. It relates to the thymus gland, circulation, and the heart and lungs.

- Imbalances in the heart chakra lead to heart disease, high blood pressure, co-dependency, and fears regarding betrayal.
- Rose, bergamot, and melissa are the essential oils associated with the heart chakra.
- The associated crystals are watermelon tourmaline, rose quartz, and emerald.
- The musical note associated with this chakra is C.
- Archangel Chamuel is the angel associated with the heart chakra.

THE THROAT CHAKRA—FIFTH CHAKRA

The throat chakra is the fifth chakra, and it is situated in the neck over the Adam's apple, directly above the thyroid gland. It vibrates the color blue, and its main issues are communication and self-expression. It is associated with the thyroid and parathyroid glands, and the mouth, throat, and ears.

- Imbalances in this chakra may result in sore throats, neck aches, problems with the thyroid, tinnitus, blocked creativity, and difficulty in expressing emotions.
- Associated essential oils include myrrh and chamomile.
- Crystals include lapis lazuli, turquoise, and aquamarine.
- The musical note associated with this chakra is D.
- Archangel Michael is the angel associated with the throat chakra.

THE THIRD EYE, OR BROW, CHAKRA—SIXTH CHAKRA

The brow chakra is the sixth chakra. It is located in the middle of the forehead, above the bridge of the nose, and is situated in front of the pituitary gland. It is also known as the "third eye" chakra. It vibrates the color indigo. Its main issues deal with intuition and wisdom. It has associations with the pituitary and pineal glands, the base of the skull, and the eyes.

- Imbalances in this chakra lead to headaches, problems with vision, learning difficulties, and nightmares.
- Associated essential oils include rose geranium and violet.

- Crystals associated with the brow chakra include amethyst, fluorite, and azurite.
- The musical note associated with this chakra is E.
- Archangel Raphael is the angel associated with the third eye chakra.

THE EAR CHAKRAS—SUB-CHAKRAS

The ear chakras are sub-chakras that affect clairaudience. Both ear chakras are positioned on the forehead above the eyebrows. They vibrate a reddish-violet shade of maroon. The ear chakras are associated with your thoughts and feelings towards hearing Divine messages. We may form blocks in our ear chakras if we have often heard harsh words, said either to us or to others. Children who live in a house where there are a lot of arguments and disharmony often close their ear chakras. If you have fears and worries regarding hearing messages from Spirit, these chakras can become dull and clouded. Ear candling is said to remove negative residue from verbal abuse and other negativity affecting the ear chakras.

- Associated essential oils include sandalwood, neroli, German chamomile, and lavender.
- The crystal associated with the ear chakras is phantom quartz.
- Archangel Jeremiel is the angel associated with the ear chakras.

THE CROWN CHAKRA—SEVENTH CHAKRA

The crown chakra is the seventh chakra and is located at the top of the head over the pineal gland. It vibrates the color violet. Its main issue focuses on spirituality. It is associated with the pineal and pituitary glands, the cerebral cortex, and the skin.

- Imbalances in this chakra may result in sensitivity to pollutants, exhaustion, confusion, obsessional thinking, and depression.
- Associated essential oils include rosewood, lavender, and frankincense.
- Crystals include amethyst, clear quartz, and diamond.
- The musical note associated with the crown chakra is F.
- Archangel Jophiel is the angel associated with the crown chakra.

Many people believe that the pineal and pituitary gland associations of the brow and crown chakras are interconnected. As the pineal sits behind and slightly higher than the pituitary, it can also be linked with the third eye. Likewise, the pituitary sits in front of the pineal, behind the brow but also below the crown, it too can be linked to the crown chakra. Both the pituitary gland of the brow and the pineal gland of the crown need to be activated in order for the third eye to open. It was once thought that the pineal gland had lost its original function due to evolution, much like the appendix. The pituitary and pineal glands are connected by a fibrous tissue forming what we can call a "psychic bridge." The pineal gland is about the size of a pea, and it is larger in children than in adults.

Developing Your Channels of Divine Communication

We all have the potential to open all four channels of psychic communication. However, it's best to start with the one with which you are more naturally in alignment. If you are predominantly clairvoyant, you will be more visually oriented. You will have a stronger auditory sense if you are clairaudient. Clairsentient people tend to be more feeling-oriented, and claircongnizant people tend to be thinkers and are often more skeptical.

There are several ways in which you can open or further develop your channels for Divine communication. It is important not to push or try too hard, as these are fear responses. With intention and practice, you will become more psychic.

CHAKRA CLEARING

The most effective way to develop or strengthen your "clairs" is to keep your chakras clear. Meditation is a good way to help to clear your chakras. There are a lot of good guided chakra meditation CDs on the market, if you find it easier to meditate this way. The key is to visualise each chakra glowing clearly and radiantly in its associated color.

DIET

Clean up your diet. Avoid caffeine and chemicals in your food. Try to eat organic fruit and vegetables. If you eat meat and fish, choose organic. Some people find that adopting a vegetarian or vegan diet helps with their Divine communication, but others don't see any difference. It's important that you adopt a diet that helps you function at optimal levels, eating whatever is ideal for you.

SOUND

Chanting or toning is very powerful. Many people believe that the sound "Om" is the sound-seed of the universe, the primordial sound. By chanting Om while focusing on your third eye area, you encourage it to open. Sometimes you might get a slight headache, but this is only due to your third eye having to work harder than usual.

In his book *Ancient Teachings for Beginners*, Douglas De Long discusses how chanting "MAAAAAY" will send a vibration deep within the head where both the pineal and pituitary glands are situated, causing these glands to vibrate, stimulating them and the surrounding areas of the brain. As a result, the crown and third eye chakras will become activated and open up.

PAY ATTENTION

Another way to develop your "clairs" is to take notice of your physical senses and concentrate on making them more acute. So if you want to develop your clairvoyance, pay more attention to the visual details of your surroundings. If you want to develop you clairaudience, pay more attention to the sound around you. Notice the sounds that you would usually block out, such as traffic or the clock ticking.

POSITIVE ENVIRONMENT

Avoiding negativity can also help you to develop your "clairs." Mix with positive people, and free your mind of negative or judgmental thoughts about yourself and others. Avoiding media and gossip magazines, and negative plays and television programs are also ways of cutting down on the amount of negativity to which you are exposed. A way to release negative energy picked up during the day is to take regular salt baths to remove energetic toxins from your body and etheric field.

I would like to finish by saying that everyone can receive Divine guidance. You don't need to be a particular type of person. We are all beautiful, perfect children of God, capable of anything we set our minds to. Happy communicating!

LUCY CHEN
SUNNYVALE, CA

Lucy Chen is a claircognizant and clairsentient whose interest in spirituality runs deep. She has studied various topics of metaphysics and spirituality for over fourteen years. She currently specializes her studies in the higher knowledge of Universal spirituality and healing.

Lucy is an ANGEL THERAPY PRACTITIONER®, certified by Doreen Virtue, Ph.D., and has been trained as a Universal White Time and Gemstone healer. She enjoys taking walks at sunset and loves cherry blossom season.

For more information or to contact Lucy, visit her website at www.sacredwings.com.

Working With the Angels

By Lucy Chen

Ever since I was a young girl, I believed in supernatural beings that lived on a different dimension on Earth. I've always held a strong belief that fairies, dragons, gnomes, and unicorns existed, despite never seeing them. All I knew was that they existed, plain and simple. On the other hand, I had heard about angels and was not sure if they were real, like the fairies, or if they were imaginary beings. To say the least, I was not interested in angels. I remember in my early years that I saw a television show about the paranormal world and there was a segment about experiences with angels. Despite my lack of interest in angels, the show made a big impact in my life because it was the first experience that introduced me to the angelic realm.

Many years later, I went to a local bookstore and asked my spiritual guides to lead me the right book. I picked up a book about fairies, and that fairy book soon lead me to books about angels and the angelic realm. To this day, I believe that angels were always around me, waiting for the right time to bring me into their world. The angels worked in subtle ways, by "seeding" information about them in my mind. They waited patiently, guiding me until I found the lessons they wanted to teach me. Of course, it took several years for me to finally realize this.

This chapter is written to help you discover how you can live your life with angels by your side, actively working with them and developing a deeper connection to them. You do not have to be a spiritual guru or a professional psychic to do this. As an ordinary person myself, I can tell you that when you open the doors to the angels, they will work with you so that you will receive messages from them. They will work with you to increase your psychic abilities and intuition. Even if you feel you do not have psychic abilities, you will receive their guidance through other ways, such as urges, dreams, or anything that you stumble across repeatedly. Be open to coincidences and take note of out of the ordinary clues and hints that the angels give, since it is very easy to dismiss these signs.

Working with angels involves understanding who they are and what they are. There are many options for learning about these heavenly helpers—attending metaphysical lectures and classes, reading books, talking to people, channeling the angels, or searching online for information.

Getting Started

A good way to start working with angels is to obtain a journal and fill it with angel information and experiences. Alternately, you can use your diary and include angel information in it to give your diary an angelic touch. The words you write and the angelic information that you receive from the angels will change the vibration of your diary.

Write down helpful information about angels and other interesting knowledge that you've read, heard, or come across. You can include poems, fill the pages with drawings, write epiphanies, jot down your thoughts and questions, and so on. Compile your own personalized encyclopedia of angel knowledge. Your journal will be one of the most handy and beloved objects that you own; you can re-read it when you want to feel comforted, happy, connected, and loved.

Angels are highly evolved spiritual beings who have extremely refined energies. When you work with them, you will notice that they can be subtle in their guidance since they are working from a higher dimension. The angels are very patient, and they are very loving, extremely helpful, and filled with joy and bliss. Your heart is warmed with just the thought of their presence.

The best angels to begin working with are your guardian angels. They have been with you since you were born and know you like a true friend.

One way to get in touch with your guardian angels is through meditation. Here is a very simple meditation that can easily be memorized and does not require recording. This meditation will help you on your way to communing with the angels. Remember to have your journal or diary nearby to record your experience.

> Find a space of rest and relaxation. This may be sitting in a comfortable chair, on the floor, or lying on your bed. Make sure you feel comfortable, and close your eyes. Take three slow, deep breaths, and relax. Concentrate on your breath as you continue to take deep breaths. Clear your mind of chatter and breathe again, relaxing even more. Take your time to really relax, since it is an important step in the meditation. Once you are in a very relaxed zone, shift your attention to the thought of wanting to meet your guardian angels. You might want to think in your mind, *I want to meet my guardian angels.* Now, let that thought linger in your mind, and feel yourself opening up your mind and heart to your guardian angels, and notice any feelings, visions, gentle voices, or urges. Take it all in, and continue to relax into that space. When you feel that you are done, slowly open your eyes.

It may take a few tries with meditation to establish a link with your guardian angels. What happens is that during your meditation, your angels realize that you want to communicate with them, and they start to test on which level they can telepathically communicate with you. It is almost like a radio station, that needs to be tuned in to discover the right frequency that works.

There are some people who groan when they hear the word "meditation" because they either have no idea how to meditate, or they fall asleep whenever they try. For those people, I recommend visual meditations because they engage the mind.

Tips for daily living with the angels

Because angels are not one hundred percent physical, it may prove a little challenging to include them in your life compared to your physical friends. Here are some tips to help you ease into a lifestyle of living with the angels:

COMMUNICATION

The easiest and the most obvious tip is to talk to your angels. Talk to your angels like you would talk to a friend. Enjoy chatting with your angels over tea or during nature walks. Angels will always listen diligently. It can be a one-sided conversation, or two-sided. If you want a two-sided conversation, then you must learn to tune in for answers. Yes and no questions are the easiest to begin with. If you are experienced with a pendulum, use it as a tool to receive answers from your angels. Alternatively, tune into their messages by going into a quiet space and allowing your mind to be in a receptive mode. Or, you can choose to meditate for their answers.

PROTECTION

Whenever you feel the need for protection, ask the angels for help. For protection and justice, many people call on Archangel Michael. Feel free to ask for many angels to be around you, protecting you, strengthening your aura from negative energies. For the visually inclined, imagine angelic white light encasing you, adding more layers of protective light around you if you feel the need for it. Angelic protection works very well in big cities and in public transportation vehicles, where you want to prevent yourself from absorbing negative energies from people. Angels can protect your home, car, family members, friends, and items, as well.

DREAM WORK

If you want to work with the angels on another level, ask them to work with you in your dreams. Ask the angels to teach you in your dreams, or you might choose to visit them in their angel ic realm for deeper healing or to remove spiritual blocks. It will take a few nights of dream work to successfully remember glimpses of your nightly activities. It does not take much effort—simply ask for what you want before going to bed. If you wake up in the morning from a surreal dream, or if you wake up very tired, even though you had enough sleep hours, you can be sure that the angels were with you.

SPIRITUAL GUIDANCE

Angels are wise and know more than we do, so naturally, asking them for spiritual guidance can prove very helpful. The best way to ask for guidance is through meditation. You can take the simple meditation from this chapter and replace the focus of the meditation to, "I need spiritual guidance in my life." We always have free will, so the angels can never force us to do something we don't want. Simply hearing that we're on the road to one destination may be all the information that we need to inspire us to change and shift the outcome. One thing that we need to keep in mind is that angels see time very differently than we do. So it is very hard to get a definite answer about when something is going to happen. Their "soon" may not be in the same time frame as your "soon." Sometimes, after asking for guidance, you'll notice that you are repeatedly hearing or seeing a particular bit of information. If that happens, it means that you are being guided and you should look into that subject.

COOKING AND DECORATING

Angels enjoy cooking and decorating. Cooking uses your creative abilities and infuses your love into the food. Angels enjoy the creative process and the infusion of love, so the next time you make dinner, invite them to help you cook! A small prayer for help and an open mind can turn your kitchen into an angel gathering place. Angels can provide inspiration to the creation of new dishes. They can make food taste better if the cooking went badly. And, they can provide company if you are the lone cook. Angels are great helpers in the household.

One of the best pieces of down-to-earth spiritual wisdom I received was from a spiritual teacher regarding home decorating. She says that a lot of people have a misconception that in order to be spiritual, we can't have material things. Her philosophy is that while we should avoid materialism, we should bring Heaven down to earth by beautifying our homes in ways that warm our souls. We can thus create our own personal versions of Heaven. Angels love beautiful presentations, just like most people, and they truly enjoy helping people decorate their homes by leading them to beautiful objects for the household.

HEALING WITH THE ANGELS

Angels are masters in the healing arts, and it is very easy to work with them to improve your health or the health of others. The angels can also assist in healing non-health problems in a variety of areas, including career, finances, relationships, event-related concerns, situational worries, and so on. If there is a prayer for healing, the angels can help, as long as it is not against your karma or your higher self's will.

There are many ways to ask for healing. The request can be spoken out loud, thought in the mind, written on paper, prayed, sung, or any other method of communication. If you want to ask in a sacred space, you can perform a sacred ceremony for healing. By performing the healing ceremony, it shows the angels your humility, respect, and effort. In the ceremony, having all the props of candles, incense, and decorations will help create a sacred space and leave you feeling very connected to the angels and the healing quality that they hold.

THE PREPARATION

Create a sanctuary for your healing request. This might be in a bedroom; clean your room and prepare your space. Cleanse your space with dried sage, which can be picked up from metaphysical shops or even a holistic health food store. Burn the sage leaves in the room and allow the smoke to cleanse away negative energies. You want your sanctuary to be positive and psychically clean.

Prepare a spot where you will sit to commune with the angels. Place a pen, paper, and unlit candles around the area. Add some angelic gemstones around you, like celestite, larimar, and angelite. Some very good healing stones I enjoy are lavender-rose quartz (for its soft energy), rose quartz (for love), chrysocolla (for bringing out repressed emotions), and carnelian (for absorbing negativity). Add nice decorations if you like, such as seashells, angel figurines, or pretty fabrics to your area. Burn incense and play some soft, healing music in the background. Your sanctuary will be waiting for you after you physically cleanse yourself.

SACRED HEALING RITUAL

You want your body to be cleansed of baggage, so that you can enter your sanctuary feeling pure. If you can do this without any health issues, take a salt bath or a salt scrub shower. Salt is cleansing, both physically and psychically. It draws physical toxins from your body and cleanses negative baggage from your aura. A regular bath or shower will do fine, too. Set your intention for being clean and pure. Imagine or feel all negative gunk flowing out of you down into Mother Earth, where she will transmute the negative energy. When you feel clean, dry yourself and step into your sanctuary.

The room should be scented with incense by now. Light the candles in your sacred space, and prepare a little prayer asking the angels to surround you and to protect this sanctuary. A favorite angel for protection is Archangel Michael. Ask for his presence here. When you feel safe and protected, continue explaining your healing request to the angels. You can direct the request to Archangel Raphael, who is the archangel of healing.

After you are done explaining, spend some time participating in the healing. Visualize how the situation is being healed and how happy you are because of it. Hold the positive visualization strongly for about five to ten minutes. Then, with the piece of paper and pen, write an affirmation. Write it three times to manifest it. Now you can keep the paper with affirmations, or you can burn the paper so that the smoke can carry your wishes to the heavens. End by thanking your angels and everyone.

WHEN YOU'RE FEELING LESS THAN ANGELIC

We all go through life in phases that can last a couple of days to several years. There are times when we hit life phases like the "I'm not spiritual" phase or the "I hate spirituality!" phase. Then sometimes, we get into the "I feel very connected to the angels" phase and then the "I am profoundly psychic" phase. I am here to tell you that it is okay to have these phases and that it is part of spiritual growth. If we felt spiritual all the time, we wouldn't get as many profound insights. So enjoy your phases, and don't berate yourself for not being "good enough."

IN CONCLUSION

Before ending this chapter, I would like to open you up to the possibilities of finding your ultimate truth. In this Universe, there is a hidden history in everything, and it will bring you to the final truth if you look deeply enough. One should never settle for anything less than the final truth, even if that means searching for the answer that is behind that answer that is behind that, that is behind that, and when you think you've reached the answer, search to see if there is an answer behind that. Ultimately, you will find *your* answer and *your* truth. But just to be sure, double check and take another look at your final answer to make sure that it really *is* final.

You'll meet more angels on

a winding path than on

a straight one.

~Daisey Verlaef

WES BLEADON-MAFFEI
NAPA AND
LOS ANGELES, CA

Wes Bleadon-Maffei, MA, is a mystic, healer, and spiritual teacher who assists people in reawakening the Christ Consciousness inherent in their soul—the consciousness of unconditional love and connection to the Divine. The essence of Wes' work is the belief that we are all expressions of love from the heart of God and that all things are healed through love and Divinity.

Not your typical spiritual teacher, Wes brings a unique blend of science and spirituality to his work, holding an MA in Natural Science and a BS in Entomology, both from San Jose State University. He is also a graduate of the University of Santa Monica with a master's degree in Spiritual Psychology.

Wes also has extensive training in a number of complementary healing and divinatory modalities including Reiki and tarot. He has studied the Kabbala with renowned Kabbalist, sociologist, and former Stanford University professor, Pamela Eakins, Ph.D. And he has studied shamanism with Alberto Villoldo, Ph.D., and Drs. Sandra and Michael Harner. He is certified in Theta Healing and is an ANGEL THERAPY PRACTITIONER® and medium, certified by Doreen Virtue, Ph.D. Wes also possesses a natural ability to communicate with animals. His website is www.soulsgrace.com.

Our Soul's Grace: Expressions of Love From the Heart of God

By Wes Bleadon-Maffei

"It matters not the way. What matters is that you are."

Loving exists and is expressed in countless ways, for it is our nature—the very essence of our soul. We do not choose to "be" love, nor do we "achieve" love—we already *are* love. We choose experiences in each lifetime that give us the opportunity to fully reveal our soul's grace and express this Divine love. We also choose our level of willingness to *be* in the loving—in other words, we choose whether or not to allow ourselves and others to experience that flow of Divine love as it is expressed through us.

Love is not just an emotion. Love cannot be fully defined with words and pictures—these are but mere labels which limit the fullness of its essence. Yet sadly, our human minds vainly try to compartmentalize and identify every form of love. In doing so, such efforts limit our ability to be fully present in the experience, making it difficult to allow Divine grace, unconditional loving, and miracles to be expressed through us.

So who—or what—helps us realize we are the very essence of love? Who is it that fills us with that innate sense of "home" we so desire? Who is it that assists us on our soul's long journey as we try to remember who we really are? Who is the shepherd that shines a light, guiding us through our darkest moments? There are, of course, many forms of Divine assistance available to humanity, but one in particular stands out as God's special messengers of grace and love: the angels.

Angels are beings of light who emanate the highest vibrations of love. They are here specifically to help us remember we are all of the light of God. They help us with our soul's experiential journey of discovery. Most of all, angels remind us we have the ability to be a bright light in the world, igniting joy and love within the souls of others.

The brief stories that follow are all true. They are token examples of how the angels send us assistance to help us remember the magic in our soul. These stories are also reminders of the Divine help we receive so that we may more easily see the expression of God's loving in the souls of others. This help can come in many forms and in many ways. The angels' influence may be obvious—a vision, a vivid dream, or an actual angelic visitation. Or their involvement may be subtle—a sudden burst of inspiration, for example, or an idea or unexpected offer of help from a friend or stranger in our time of need.

I shall begin with the story of Mattie, a beautiful person whose life was filled with many great challenges. I met Mattie just before Christmas at a hospital a few years ago when my father was battling to survive a systemic infection of *Staphylococcus* bacteria. My father was in a room on the first floor of the hospital, having a procedure done. My mother and I were waiting anxiously in the waiting room, praying and hoping.

During our wait, I heard what sounded like piano music coming from the foyer down the hall. A missed note here, a clinker there, and I began to wonder: *Who is trying to play that Christmas music and having so much trouble? Why is this being allowed?* Sadly, not all of my thoughts were charitable, and my ego stepped in. Having the gifts of perfect pitch and the ability to play the piano, I went to investigate. What I found was a scrawny, gray-haired, hunched-over, middle-aged woman whose hands were struggling to play *O Holy Night*, one of my favorite Christmas songs. At that moment, she was playing this part of the song: *Fall on your knees, Oh hear the Angels' voices!*

Mattie completed the song, stopped, and looked up to see who was watching. There was a twinkle in her eye, and a slight smile of recognition crept over her face as our eyes met. In that instant I felt this huge presence, and all I could see was an unusually bright light around this woman. We struck up a conversation, and I learned she had been coming to this hospital for the last few years during the Christmas season to "bring more joy to those in need." The more we talked, the more enchanted I became.

I asked her if she took requests. "Of course," she replied, "but no one has ever stopped to ask me that before. What would you like to hear?" I asked to hear another favorite, *Ave Maria*. As if possessed, she began to play, and this time, she didn't miss a single note. In fact, every song thereafter was played to perfection, with a heavenly sound I had never heard before and I haven't heard since. When it was time for me to leave, she thanked me for our time together and told me this was the first time in all the years she had been playing at the hospital, other people had stopped and noticed. "You have given me a beautiful gift," she said.

My total time with Mattie was just under forty minutes. In that time, I too had been given a great gift, although it would be much later before I fully realized it. The truth is my heart had been touched by an angel who reminded me that I, too, was filled with grace—that only Divine love is real. And even the tiniest act of kindness can make all the difference to someone in need.

I left Mattie that day never to see her again. I will never forget her and the magic exchanged between our two souls. I later learned from a local nurse that Mattie was both mentally and physically challenged—this was why her speech was sometimes hard to understand and her appearance a bit bedraggled. Mattie never knew her parents, as they had left her at the State Institution for special needs people and unwanted children when she was born, never to see her again. I further learned it was very late in her life before anyone took the time to teach her basic life skills such as speaking, walking, being hygienic, eating, and being in the presence of others. She had been, in essence, a forgotten member of a society that did not really know what to do with her. Mattie passed away in 2005.

No less remarkable is the story of Miguel, a postal carrier whose heartfelt desire has always been to bring light and joy into the lives of others.

Miguel is an individual I have known for many years. He is a rather unassuming middle-aged man whose postal carrier job is equally as unglamorous. His life is simple, and he does not ask for very much. Each week, he sorts, carries, and delivers the mail, bringing with it a smile and loving hello. He admits his early childhood was very challenging—he did not finish high school or go to college, and like many, he has been through divorce, bankruptcy, and other hardships. Through it all, he has lived each day fulfilling his unexplainable heartfelt dream of wanting to make the world a brighter place.

It was December of 2006 when I first learned of the latest miracles Miguel was working in the lives of those less fortunate. I already knew he was working to help teenagers in trouble with the law find purpose and value in their lives. I did not know he was a real-life Santa Claus during the holiday season. And not just any old Santa Claus, like those we find in department stores or on street corners. I mean Santa Claus, just like in the stories of old.

On the afternoon of December 24, I called Miguel to wish him a Merry Christmas. He promptly informed me he was very busy and under any other circumstances, he would love to chat. Thinking he was behind in his shopping, I began to rib him a little. Soon I discovered I was way off the mark.

He told me he had a secret, and because of the season and his feelings of generosity, he was willing to share it with me. What he told me was astonishing—he was busy filling hundreds of stockings with goodies and small treats. He would be delivering them throughout that night to needy families that were unable to do much, if anything, for their children because of their present circumstances.

This "Divine inspiration," as he described it, found him following the completion of a rather hostile and messy divorce at the start of the holiday season, nine years ago. While grieving his loss and grappling with his fears of possible financial ruin, "a little voice out of nowhere" reminded him how Christmas had always been, and would continue to be, his favorite holiday. The voice then reminded him further that Divine love came from within and that he felt the greatest joy when he was of service, bringing joy to others. Christmas, he was told, is the time of year to celebrate and remember love and joy are with us throughout the year, no matter where we are or what we are doing.

It was then and there that inspiration found him. He remembered playing Santa many years earlier in another city and how much he had loved it. He claimed that everything simply fell into place as if some great force was at work, masterfully coordinating each and every step along the way. First he remembered from his postal routes which families had little, if anything, to celebrate Christmas with and compiled a list. He was then guided to go to the local stores (WalMart, Target, Plaza Jet Supermart, Dollar Tree, and Stan's Merry Mart). There, he literally asked the employees what sort of deal would they make him for the stockings, candies, and small toys he would buy in bulk on Christmas Eve. He explained what he was doing for the needy families, and lo and behold, they not only gave him a substantial discount on the candies, they donated the toys and stockings! Finally, as if on cue, he found a red, seventeenth-century Catholic cardinal's robe and hat at an estate sale for only a few dollars. To say the least, I was amazed by Miguel's story.

He went on to say that at first, there were only a few families. This year he was delivering gifts to over four hundred families in six different communities! He discovered most of these families through word-of-mouth. They did not know he was coming and would never know from whom the gifts came. The few who did know he was coming would usually be waiting, wanting to see him in his deep red robes and visit for a few minutes before he left the stockings behind. He would travel to many rural towns on Christmas Eve, driving hundreds of miles through the snow and ice in his broken-down jalopy.

Not knowing what to say, I expressed my amazement and apologized. He graciously accepted and closed our discussion by telling me his only reason for doing this was to give each family and their children a lasting memory of joy on what would otherwise be a potentially joyless day. He said, "It warms my heart to know when people open their doors not expecting anything, they find someone cared. I love celebrating Christmas in this way, knowing it helps rekindle people's faith in their fellow man. And most of all, I believe these types of memories provide hope and help people remember they, too, are special and of value."

Mattie and Miguel share one thing in common—an angelic presence in their lives. Whether they were actually in the presence of angels, being assisted by angels, or being guided by the angels to assist others, the individuals in these stories demonstrate how the angels provide exactly what we need for our own growth and upliftment, in every way imaginable.

Furthermore, the angels help orchestrate those experiences, which further connect us with who we really are. And of course, who we are is love—pure Divine God love, the essence of grace.

So how do we connect with God, the angels, and our Divine essence of love? The connection starts with a wish or a question:

What if...
Wouldn't that be nice?
My, I would love to...

We can invoke the help of God and the angels any time, no matter what is happening in our lives—even during our darkest hours. Many times, we call on God and the angels without even realizing it. Yes, we can directly ask for something, being very specific. But most of the time, we beseech God and the angels for assistance indirectly, without a lot of specificity:

God help me.
Oh my God!
Help!
God grant me grace.
Oh God, what do I do now?
I do not understand.
Wouldn't it be nice if...

These are all indirect ways of asking for what we are truly desiring in our heart of hearts.

Allowing ourselves to receive is also an important part of our soul's evolutionary process. This is essential—without such willingness, we miss the many opportunities of assistance that have been brought before us. We need to be mindful of the fact that what we are given may not look like what we were asking for. Usually, it's *more* than we knew to ask for! And many times the full value of the assistance reveals itself only after we have allowed ourselves to receive and be grateful for what we were given.

There are times, however, when it appears our requests go unanswered. But do not be misled—even in these circumstances, we have truly been given what we need for our highest and best good. In these instances, we may already have exactly what we need. If this is not the case, it could be that our request has conflicting elements. And it is also possible we are blocking our ability to receive. In these instances, our ability to listen and attune to the gift(s) of our present experience as guidance becomes important. For, from this place, we are able to gracefully acknowledge and receive what our soul, and the angels have conspired to give us. And it is in our allowing, our willingness to receive, that we help create those experiences guiding us towards a deeper sense and understanding of who we are and our purpose.

What this all boils down to is choice. We have free will to choose what we want, those we spend our lives with, and how we will interact with our world. In our choices, we create the experiences which bring us closer to realizing *we* are what we have always been seeking. We are the very love and grace that we desire. The angels and other Divine helpers who work with us simply bring to us the tokens of magic which guide and help us remember. When we ask, we open the door of opportunity to fully understand "It matters not the way, what matters is that you are."

Remember:

- Be willing to dream. Allow your imagination to talk with you and teach you. It is safe to dream. This is a key part of your guidance system.

- Ask the angels for assistance. They are standing by, eager to help.

- Ask for what you desire and let it further guide you in clarifying what you want.

- Focus on the feeling of already having received your desire by saying, "Wouldn't it be nice if…" This is much more powerful and supportive than the feeling of want, which tends to energize consciousness of lack.

- Allow yourself to receive what you have asked for.

- Assistance comes in many forms and is expressed in many ways. Be open to the possibility that what you have asked for may show up and be different than anything you could have imagined at the time.

- Be grateful for what you already have, as this enhances the flow of goodness in your life and the lives of others.

- Our experiences are an expression of loving, which serve to nurture and remind us who we are and why we are here.

- You have a limitless capacity for love that resides within you, for you are an expression of love from the heart of God.

MELISSA FEICK
SEVERENA PARK, MD

M elissa Feick, ANGEL THERAPY PRACTITIONER®, has a healing and angel practice in Maryland. She helps people of all ages to rediscover their full potential and find their inner guidance. Melissa has a Bachelor of Science degree in Psychology and constantly studies to become familiar with different healing modalities in order to assist others on their life paths. She is married and a mother of two beautiful children. She became an aunt at the age of seven, and has been around children her whole life. When Melissa was in seventh grade, she decided that she was going to college to become a child psychologist.

Although fate had other plans, Melissa feels that she is truly living her life purpose by being of service to adults and children. You may contact her by writing to her at Empower The Light Within, 820 Ritchie Highway, Suite 225, Severna Park, MD 21146, by visiting her website at www.EmpowerTheLightWithin.com, or by email, at Melissa@EmpowerTheLightWithin.com.

The Intuitive Child

By Melissa Feick

eing blessed with two wonderful children and having observed many parents and educators interacting with children of all ages, I have come to the realization that it is in our best interest to understand and properly guide the children of today. The terms Indigo, Crystal, and Rainbow children describe today's intuitive children. These young masters are the next creative, loving beings that will be in charge of the earth and her inhabitants in the future. It is my understanding that there have always been special children, prodigies, and kids with a solid connection to God. Today there are either more of them or we are becoming more aware of them. Either way, they are here. The question is, how can we help, encourage, and love them unconditionally?

As educators, parents, grandparents, friends, and neighbors, it is up to us to encourage and notice the sensitive children that have graced us with their presence. It would be nice if we could accept these beauties for who and what they are: gifts from God/Creator. And aren't we lucky to know these little angels?

I have been told who and what God is from many different sources. My parents, teachers, ministers, and priests have all tried to tell me everything they know about God from what the Bible says. Though these adults have tried their best to guide me toward a relationship with God, being around children has shown me the truth for which God stands. In their eyes is a wisdom and connection to the Creator I have come to admire. Ask a young child about God and the answers are usually more insightful than anything you will learn from the "experts." The more open we are to these little beings, the more open we are to the creative Source of the All. As adults, it is our privilege to learn from this race of young Lightworkers. We are working for them, they are teaching us, and we are all evolving together.

The spiritual child is usually a sensitive soul with a great grasp of the true reality. From the young age of two to around five or six, they see the world more through God's eye than society's eye. They notice and become excited about some very interesting things. It is that childlike curiosity that helps them explore the world around them without the constraints of society and its expectations. The spiritually sensitive child has some particular needs of which we all need to be aware.

The Sensitive Child

From a very young age, I was an extremely sensitive child. According to my family, being sensitive was not acceptable; I cried too much for them and was told I was too dramatic. I lived in a busy household with four older siblings who were preteens and teenagers when I was quite young. A lot of hormonal energy ruled the house, and my mother was always working hard. With so many emotions and issues happening around me, and being the only young child in the house, I tended to be a loner. By the time I was eight, everyone but my teenaged brother was out of the house. I was raised like an only child and spent many hours a day outside in the woods, at the pond, or playing alone at home. I remember trying to make friends, but I never felt like I fit in; nature was my friend.

I was clairsentient as a child. Most clairsentients have trouble distinguishing their emotions from others' feelings. They are affected by the energies of others and may even mimic their behaviors. If someone is angry, the clairsentient may start to feel angry and they do not even know why. Many clairsentients become withdrawn; the world is too harsh for them. I have noticed that many children are clairsentient. As babies, these children will cry when an alcoholic, drug addict, or someone who is depressed tries to hold them—particularly if their parents are clear of lower energies. If the child is used to positive energy, the lower energy is foreign to them, and crying is a rejection of the lower energy. These children can feel the difference between the higher and lower vibrations. The sensitive child has trouble distinguishing their feelings from others. A person with very strong anger, depression, or any other lower frequency can adversely affect the child.

Sensitive children tend to reflect the energy of those around them. Clairsentient children need extra attention and protection. As caregivers, we need to be aware of negative influences because they will affect sensitive children more than other children. If they are belittled, yelled at often, or told they are too sensitive, they will start to shut down their clairsentience and natural intuition.

In one of my psychology classes, we talked at length about experiments that created desensitized people. The fastest and easiest way to desensitize someone is by exposing him or her to violent images. People were shown images of men, women, and children being killed, blown up, and tortured. In the beginning their heart would race and their blood pressure would rise. After repeated exposure to these grotesque images, their reactions became less and less significant. They got used to the images. If you are interested in exposing the children in your life to the spiritual world, you are better off leaving the violent video games and movies in the store. Those types of images serve no purpose for the insightful child, and there are plenty of non-violent activities out there for them to enjoy. In order for children to develop compassion, they need to be sensitive to the needs, difficulties, and problems of others, not aloof or desensitized to suffering.

Being a clairsentient myself, I know how one can be affected by this psychic ability. When I was a young teen, I had trouble watching violent movies, but as I got older, I started to watch and love action movies and horror flicks. I started not being bothered at all. Actually, I started to need more and more violence to get my adrenaline pumping. Also, as I aged, I was taught that crying was a bad thing, and I became more and more angry as I suppressed my emotions. When I started my spiritual path, I started watching fewer violent movies. Now those movies are much too charged for me and make me feel sick. I like being clairsentient because when I am with a client I can feel their pain without taking it on, and I am more compassionate.

Protection

Clairsentients go out into the world with all of their "feelers" out. They feel the world and the people they come in contact with. Because they are so open, some form of protection would be of great benefit to them. As babies and little children, they have a natural form of protection. By the time they start to walk with confidence and really explore their world, those defenses weaken and energy starts to impact them more and more.

Many in the spiritual community talk about lower energies and entities that attach themselves to the auric field. Children have a natural defense against entities, but the lower energies of others can affect them, especially once they hit school age, around five years old. It is important to protect school-aged children especially from the energy of others. I watch my nine-year-old with his friends and notice that when he is around very intense, active children, he changes and his energy changes. He is much more hyperactive, tends not to think things through, and gets into more trouble. He picks up the other children's energy and mimics it.

Little ones can also pick up on our moods and emotions. When a parent is depressed, the child starts to become depressed, especially a sensitive child. Protection from these energies is easy; just put a bubble of light around them. Remember Glenda the good witch from the *Wizard of Oz*? She came down from the sky in a perfect clear bubble. That is what your bubble of protective energy should look like in your mind's eye. It can be a bubble of any color—white, gold, or pink are especially good. This light is from God and can be used at any time. I see it surrounding my children every morning. In her book, *Angel Medicine*, Dr. Doreen Virtue describes the use of different colored bubbles and how they help to protect. I use different colors as needed, but for the most part, I just use the white and gold light on my children. I was taught to say a prayer when I bubble and it can be as short or as long as needed. I say something like, "Connor is surrounded by God's pure light and is protected always." Or "Connor is protected and safe."

We have two cars and our children ride in both of them, so these are bubbled, too. When we plan to be around a lot of people, like at fairs or in airports, I place extra bubbles around them. I talk to my nine-year-old about bubbling, but I still do it for him, as he does not always remember to do so, and it is my job as his mother!

Every day, my children get onto the bus to go to school. Their bus driver is very nice, but her driving always makes me nervous, so I started bubbling the bus and filling it with angels every day. The bus was involved in an accident at the beginning of the school year. Luckily, there were no children on board at the time. I thanked God and the angels for protecting the children who rode that bus because I know the bubble and angels saved lives that day.

I also fill the school up with angels—I figure it can't hurt and can only help! In addition, I enlist the loving help of the fairies. However, I advise them to hang out outside and only fool around during recess.

Our home is always bubbled to protect against lower energies. The loving fairies and other elementals, angels, and guides are allowed access. They are so much fun to have around! On a daily basis, I either clear the house of lower energies by using God's light or Archangel Michael. God's light fills the whole home, including the corners, behind and under things, between walls, attics, and all space in between. It outshines anything that is not for our highest good. I call in Archangel Michael to clear the house of all lower energy, from top to bottom, inside and out, so that it can be safe for our family. The clearer and brighter the energy, the safer everyone feels.

As a parent, it is hard to let your child go out into a world where you do not know what is going on. But it has to happen, where all we can do is pray, protect, and send angels with them! I also feel that if my children are well adjusted and know that they are loved, they will be fine because we create our reality. In my reality, my children are always safe!

Nightmares

It is interesting that both of my children went through a stage of nightmares. The dreams affected them deeply. I remember feeling so alone and unprotected after a nightmare, and I do not want my children to feel the same way.

In our house, we love to talk about our dreams. Dreams are so important to your psychological health and well-being. They are a great way to gain insight into your children, too. Once in a while my little one will tell me that she was left alone in a dream—we all left her and something bad was going to get her. At times, her dreams reflect this feeling of abandonment. She is always clingy with me and does not like me leaving. I know she is tapping into a past life where she was either abandoned, people she loved were killed, or she was killed. I tell her she has control of her dreams, not the other way around. I also tell her she can change her dreams whenever she needs so they are not so scary.

This did not console her enough, though, so we started calling Archangel Michael to protect her through the night. (Yes, AA Michael is a very busy angel in our home, but since he is omnipresent, meaning he can be everywhere anytime, he can do this in every home across the earth and beyond!) I say something like "AA Michael, please watch over Kyra through the night, guard all the doors and windows so no lower energies can come through, and protect her in her dreams. Help her to understand that she can control her own dreams and that she is safe." She likes to add "and no bad dreams, just good dreams!" I figure whatever makes her happy and able to sleep easier is great for everyone!

I like to talk with my children soul to soul while they are asleep. With the nightmares my little one was having, I started going in there and saying, "Kyra, you can control your own dreams. You are in control, and you can change your dreams whenever you want." Kyra was asking for a unicorn Pegasus to come into her dream, and after one or two nights of nighttime conditioning she came running into me one morning all excited because she changed her dream and rode a unicorn Pegasus! What a great confirmation for both of us!

I also go in their room sometimes and just say things like "I love you," "You are a wonderful person," "I am so proud of you," "You are kind and gentle," or anything else that feels right. If they have had a difficult day, I try to say uplifting things to them. Of course, I tell them these things while awake, too; I just feel it is an added bonus if they know it on a deeper level. When Connor was around two years old, he would get stressed when friends would come over to play. He thought that if they played with his toys, they would take them home. I started nighttime conditioning, saying "You have a great time when your friends come to play. You love to share your toys. They will play with your toys with you and leave them here when they leave." I have been thinking about telling them that they LOVE PEAS AND CARROTS, so maybe they will be asking for peas for a snack instead of cookies!

One day, my sister mentioned that her son of about four was having night terrors. He would wake up in the middle of the night very scared and inconsolable. During the day, he was worried about his mother leaving him. A little while later, he spent the night at our house. He and Connor were very close. After he left, Connor told me that his cousin said that the soldiers took his mother and sister away and that they were going to get him. It was then that I realized what was causing his night terrors—it was some sort of memory, and a large part of him did not know that he was in a different time and place. This is called cellular memory, when our cells hold onto either a past life or a genetic memory. I told my sister what Connor had relayed to me. I suggested that she talk to her son, Thomas (not his real name) about this memory in as much detail as he would give. I explained how to reassure him that he was safe and that neither she nor his sister was going anywhere. I also suggested that for the next few nights she talk to him in his sleep. This way his unconscious mind could start to understand that the memory was from another lifetime before he was Thomas, and that he is safe, that everyone he loved is safe. She assured him that she was not going anywhere and that she would never leave him. Although he still is a restless sleeper and has nightmares, my nephew's night terrors seem to be under control.

As a spiritual advisor, I have worked with concerned parents, grandparents, and others to help them to cope with the dynamics of the sensitive child. There is so much to learn and understand, I am constantly trying to find ways to work with these children. The most important thing I have discovered so far is that, as a parent, I have made mistakes, but I always try to do my best. Be gentle with both yourself and your children— we are all here to experience this reality together. What a blessing!

Babies are angels whose

wings grow shorter as their

legs grow longer.

~Anonymous

RHONDA COLLINS
CLUNES, VICTORIA
AUSTRALIA

Born February 1, 1951, in Melbourne, Australia, Rhonda Collins grew up in a fairly traditional Australian household. She left school at the age of fifteen and went on to become a hairdresser.

At age thirty-one, she began teacher training. She taught various subjects and then went on to complete a course in teaching English as a second language.

Rhonda holds a master of education degree in adult vocational education and training, a postgraduate degree in educational studies, a postgraduate diploma of education (computers in education), and she has almost completed a second masters degree in Teaching English to Speakers of Other Languages. Rhonda is about to commence a Ph.D. program studying the education of Indigo and Crystal children and young adults.

Rhonda is an Angel Intuitive™ with advanced training, certified by Doreen Virtue, Ph.D. She truly loves working with the angelic realm, calling on the angels whenever advice or guidance is required.

Contact Rhonda for readings via email at rcollin3@bigpond.net.au, or by visiting Rhonda's website at www.anangelonmyshoulder.com.au.

Working with the Angelic Kingdom

By Rhonda Collins

The night my beautiful pet bird Joey died, I had my first encounter with the angels. I was seven years old, lying fast asleep in my bed. The room was dark and the house very still. Suddenly, I was awakened by the sound of a choir singing! Startled, I sat bolt upright and listened to the distinctive sound. It was truly beautiful.

Even though the music was wonderful, I was deeply frightened—too scared to go back to sleep.

"Mom! Dad!" I called to my parents, rousing them from their sleep.

"What is it, Rhonda?" my mother asked from her room across the hall.

"Can't you hear that music?" I asked her. It was so loud! Surely she could hear it.

"I don't hear anything, Rhonda. Go back to sleep," she replied.

I rolled over in my bed, pulling the covers over my head. I felt certain and knew in my heart that the singing was coming from a choir of angels. Eventually sleep returned, but when I woke the next morning, I found Joey dead in his cage.

Although deeply upset at the death of Joey, it was reassuring to know that the angels had taken his spirit with them, and although I was too young to understand how special it was to have heard the angelic choir accompanying my feathered friend as he passed over, I was at peace because he was not alone.

Over the years, I have had an affinity with birds and have held them in my hands as they made their transition, feeling honoured by the fact that they have chosen me to be with them at their passing.

As I got older, I went to school to become a hairdresser; a few years later, I chose to return to academia. It was not going to be easy—I would have to leave from work and drive an hour and a half in heavy traffic to attend classes twice a week. During many of my trips, I was aware that I was not travelling alone. I felt as though I had someone with me, protecting me on my journey. Whenever I got into the car for the commute to school, I would silently wish that my journey would be safe, that I would find a good place to park my car, and that I would make it to my class on time. The area was dangerous at night, so a well-lit parking spot in close proximity to my class was a necessity.

My prayers were definitely heard. Every red light turned green just as I approached, traffic was heavy but flowed smoothly, and almost always, I would find just the right car park...just my angels behind the scenes, orchestrating things so that they flowed smoothly.

When I was about twenty-eight years old, I began having prophetic dreams. One such dream involved my father and my two young daughters. In the dream, I saw most clearly a vehicle slamming into my father's car. The impact of the accident spun his car around, causing the other vehicle to strike my father's car once again, this time on the opposite side. I then saw the bodies of my two daughters in the back seat—they were both dead. The rear passenger doors had gaping holes of jagged metal.

My father was due to take my girls to visit a relative who was dying of leukemia. At the last minute, my father decided not to take the girls with him. Going to the hospital, a woman ran a red light, sending my father's car spinning into cars waiting to turn. Both rear doors ended up with gaping holes; had the girls been in their usual seats, they would have been killed. My father was uninjured.

I had told my mother about my dream, and I can only imagine that was the reason why my father changed his mind and decided to leave my daughters at home.

Incidents such as this brought me to the realization that *something* was happening, but I still wasn't thinking angels.

The next event happened one afternoon whilst I was having a brief nap. My girls were playing out front, riding their bikes with their father supervising them. When I nodded off, I began to dream. My dream saw the man next door reversing much too quickly out of his driveway. I heard a scream from my elder daughter as his car struck her.

I was awakened from my dream by my husband carrying my elder daughter into the house. It seems that the girls were riding their bikes on the footpath when a little boy swerved to avoid being hit by the neighbor's rapidly reversing car. The boy's bike hit my daughter.

Another prophetic dream occurred some weeks later when I dreamt of a plane landing across from where we lived, in the sixty-five acres of parkland. No one appeared injured in my dream. On arriving home from work several days later, I was met by many emergency vehicles and television news crews spread across the roadway. Upon closer inspection, I saw a light aircraft crashed in the parkland across from our house. Fortunately no one was injured.

I began to fear going to sleep in case I dreamt of things that were too horrendous to think about. My friends at work were calling me a "white witch." I had made the mistake of telling them about my dreams. It was a name that really bothered me. On one occasion, my workplace was to hold a fundraising event on a Saturday. We had had a week of rain, and because part of the event was to be outdoors, my work friends taunted me with "Come on, you're a white witch. Make the rain stop for Saturday." The rain was heavy all day on the Friday and during that night, but come Saturday morning, the rain had stopped and the sun was shining. Although I had nothing to do with the weather change, the taunts of "white witch" just grew worse, making me regret having told them of my dreams in the first place.

It was about this time that I decided I didn't want to know anything further and shut down whenever I began to receive intuitive messages or dreams.

I knew I wasn't the only one in my family to receive psychic messages. There has always been a strong link between members of my family and the angelic realm and spirit world. I have had many relatives on my mother's side of the family that have had spiritual encounters, and whenever my mother has been seriously ill, her deceased mother comes and sits beside her bed, giving her comfort and guidance.

My mother also has an inner knowing that I know to be her angels. When she gets "a feeling" that something is going to happen, it usually does. She also gets a "feeling" about certain people. She is usually accurate when that happens, too.

My two daughters also have strong spiritual links. They reported astral travelling when they were as young as six and seven. They were also aware of spirits within their bedrooms. They were able to describe them to me in great detail.

All of this evidence and support couldn't convince me to open up completely to the world of the angels, however. I didn't revisit my spiritual self until a few years ago when I had a very close call with death.

My father, whom I loved most dearly, was deteriorating rapidly physically. He was forced to use oxygen to help him to breathe and was unable to talk very much because he was so short of breath. I knew that he didn't have that much longer to live, but I didn't want to face that fact.

Although my life had been really difficult and a struggle at times, something had always come along to brighten things up for me; this time there wasn't a miracle to magically restore my father's health.

Seeing my father suffering, the thought of losing him—these things were too much to bear. I began to slip into a downward spiral of depression and desperation. I could see no end to the pain in sight. I just wanted the hurt and fear to go away. I knew just one way to do that: suicide. I took three overdoses of pain medication in two weeks. The strange thing was that I didn't really want to die; I just wanted to wake up and have everything be all right again. However, I almost ended my life. My elder daughter, who was six months pregnant at the time, was advised by the doctors to place me into a psychiatric hospital for a short time to get me back on track. It was there that my angels took me in hand.

The first two days in hospital, I was unconscious. After I woke up, they transferred me from the High Dependency ward and to a room of my own in the general area of the hospital. I was having severe seizures at that point; during one of the seizures, I had a strong desire to "talk" to my angels. It was like a light had been switched on. The despair came pouring from me. I spoke to my angels of my sense of utter helplessness, expressing how unbelievably petrified I was at the thought of my father dying. At one point, I recall someone entering my room, sitting on the bed, and holding my hand. A sense of warmth, then peace flowed through me. I then knew I was going to be all right. At first I thought my visitor had been a nurse or fellow patient, but after satisfying myself that neither had occurred, I became certain that my visitor was from the angelic realm.

The night before my father passed over, I asked my angels to please take him quickly so that he wouldn't suffer anymore. I wasn't at all surprised when the next day, the phone call came through that my father had passed away peacefully. I left the psychiatric hospital to attend his funeral. Several days later, I was drifting off to sleep when I felt a strong tug, first on my arm, then on my bed clothes. I knew it was my father, coming to say goodbye. I saw the room light up with a golden glow. I felt peace and love fill my bedroom. My father was letting me know that all was well and he was safe. As a child, when my father needed to wake me from sleep, he would tug gently at my arm. My dad was tugging more noticeably this time to really get my attention. He just knew that I would recognise that it was him by his actions.

My daughter gave birth to her daughter three months to the date after my father died. My granddaughter has my father's personality and many of his ways.

Since my suicide attempt, the angels have used me as a tool for helping and healing other people—it's quite simply part of my Divine mission, the work that I came to earth to do. Today I work with the angelic realm every day, and I listen to the messages I receive. Every message given to me is very important and gives me instructions to follow. Typically, the angels' messages lead me in just the right direction at just the right time.

When a close family member had a problem with gambling, on several occasions, I received messages telling me to go to a certain location where I would find this person gambling. Even when I strongly doubted this person would be there, I followed my angels, and they were always correct. Although it saddened me greatly to find this family member gambling, it allowed me to sit and talk with the person and find out what had triggered the gambling on that occasion.

Sometimes my messages from the angels come to me as a strong "knowing."

My (now deceased) second husband was a flight attendant with an international airline. He had been a very heavy smoker but had chosen to give up cigarettes about nine weeks before he was due to fly to London.

He rang me from London when he arrived—it was then that I had my strong sense of knowing. I told him that he had been smoking, to which he answered that he had smoked only one cigarette; he was curious to know how I had found out. I never did tell him that my angels tattled on him!

On a more serious note, a few years later he was working in another industry and was working an early shift. It was my habit to ring him when he arrived home from work each day. On this occasion I rang him at the usual time, but he wasn't at home. I rang a second and third time, but the angels had already told me what was wrong—he had suffered a stroke, but would be okay. I chose to disbelieve them.

When he had been missing for nine and a half hours, I had to listen to the angels. The stroke had made him confused—he had wandered for hours, not knowing where he was, or even where he lived. He had managed to board a bus, which took him miles from our home. In his confusion, he had gone to a stranger's house several suburbs away, and then tried to open their front door with his own front door key. These people took him inside and gave him water, but rang the police because they could see he wasn't acting normally. It took many months for him to recover.

Eighteen months after the first stroke, he had a second, more debilitating stroke. This time he was in a wheelchair for about two years, and then he slowly recovered enough to get around in a motorized scooter. He lived in relatively poor health from 1990 until his death from a heart attack in 2004. He was sixty-one.

I was with him in Palliative Care when he passed over. I was sleeping in a chair in his room when something woke me and told me to go to him. I placed my hand on his shoulder as he inhaled deeply. It was his last breath. I felt at peace because I was aware of his angels there in the room, ready to take him with them. The angels supported me throughout that entire event.

During the past twelve months, I have asked the angels for direction with my life. I have asked many times, in fact. They have told me often to be patient and to trust. I know in my heart that their words are true and that I must take their advice, but it is often more difficult to put into practice than one would think.

Late last year, I received word from the angels that I must work with the Indigo and Crystal children and other young people. The thought of working with these young people was something that I knew I would enjoy, but I also knew it would be a challenge. My main concern, though, was how to start this work—I had no idea how to proceed. I asked the angels for advice, but they just told me to be patient.

I looked at completing Steiner teacher education, but that didn't resonate. I scanned the Internet, but found nothing that jumped out at me to say "This is it."

In January of 2007, I received the word from the angels that I was to go to the university. It was not the university where I had completed my other studies; however their message was clear—go to the university near my home.

I went to the university where I met with a former lecturer of mine. He was able to introduce me to the right people who just happened to be interested in my topic for a Ph.D. The topic is "Educating Indigo and Crystal children and young adults."

My supervisor has a daughter who is an Indigo, and she has worked in special education for many years. I still marvel at the serendipitous flow of events as my path continues to unfold before me.

Nonetheless, I suspect that the issue of trust has made my path more difficult than it has to be. The angels keep telling me to trust them and to have faith, but that is one of the hardest things to do! They haven't let me down so far, though, so my trust issues are disappearing slowly.

I have always loved anything to do with angel statues, books, paintings, cards, etc., but never quite knew why. It is my strong belief that my angels have been knocking on my door since I was very little, but my stubbornness prevented me from seeing their signs. I am truly glad that I finally got the message and began to listen to them because they really have changed my life completely.

If trouble hearing angels' song
with thine ears, try listening with
thy heart.

~Meriel Stelliger

VALERIE CAMOZZI
MARIN COUNTY, CA

Valerie Camozzi is a gifted clairvoyant, founder of Light Resonance Healing®, and author of the forthcoming book, *Mom, I Want to go There*, a world seen through the eyes of a psychic child. She is an intuitive reader, public speaker, holistic energy practitioner, and a registered yoga teacher. Valerie is an ANGEL THERAPY PRACTITIONER®, certified by Doreen Virtue, Ph.D., and a certified medium and professional spiritual teacher. Valerie has studied with master teachers throughout the United States and internationally and has been teaching classes about angels, healing, and spirituality in the San Francisco Bay area, throughout the U.S., and internationally since 1995.

She provides teleconferences, workshops, and private consultations with clients. Her ability to connect with Spirit on multiple levels has been an important part of her life and work. Valerie uses her gifts and abilities to help others connect with Spirit by teaching them how to develop their own intuitive abilities to work with the angelic and spiritual realms, and how to receive information and guidance from these realms. Valerie travels to sacred places such as Egypt and Machu Picchu, Peru. She takes groups to sacred sites to connect with and experience the light and wisdom these places hold. These journeys provide an opportunity for growth that allows both personal and planetary transformation to occur.

As a California teacher holding both Multiple Subjects and Developmentally Disabled teaching credentials, Valerie taught severely handicapped children and adults, and worked as a registered nurse in neonatal and pediatric intensive care for twenty-five years. For more information about Valerie, go to www.luminousoul.com, or email valcamozzi@comcast.net.

Angelic Birth Experiences

By Valerie Camozzi

An Answered Prayer

I work in the newborn intensive care unit as a registered nurse. As a part of my job, I attend all deliveries that are considered to be high risk. High risk means that the baby is not responding well to the mother's contractions during labor. The obstetrician is the one that makes the decision if a newborn intensive care team should be present at the delivery to assist the infant. The team usually includes a physician, a nurse, and a respiratory therapist. On occasion, the decision is made to have the newborn intensive care nurse on standby in the room without the rest of the team. Such was the case recently, when I arrived at work and was called immediately to a delivery room. The obstetrician wanted to be cautious in this situation and provide extra care for the newborn, if needed, but she felt that she wouldn't need the whole team. The mother's labor was progressing nicely, and the baby's heart rate was within normal range. I prepared the warming bed and equipment for the infant's arrival. The warming bed is where the infant is placed immediately after delivery so that he or she can be examined. As I waited for the baby to be born, I heard a voice in my head telling me to call a doctor from the NICU to join me at the birth.

At first I thought it was my imagination, but the voice repeated the message, again telling me to have a doctor join me during the delivery. I turned to the obstetrician and told her that I would feel more comfortable if a physician from the NICU joined me in the delivery room. The obstetrician said there was clearly no indication to warrant having the physician join me as the mother's labor was progressing normally and the baby's heart rate continued to be within normal range.

Just as the baby's head was crowning and the delivery had begun, the voice came again repeating that a physician from the NICU should be brought in for this delivery. I said a quiet prayer asking that a physician from my unit be outside the delivery room door.

When the baby was born, his color was dark blue, indicating that he wasn't getting enough oxygen. I took the baby from the obstetrician and placed him on the warming bed, immediately giving him oxygen as I dried him off. I informed the obstetrician that I needed to take the infant to the NICU. I placed the identification bracelet on the infant, let the mother and father see their son, and then whisked him out the door and off to my unit. Standing right outside the door of the delivery room was a physician from my unit, who took one look at the infant and followed me to the newborn intensive care unit. My prayer had been answered. As the two of us entered the NICU with the baby, we were joined by the other members of the team, and we went to work on the infant to stabilize him. The infant was stabilized and then transferred to another facility that specialized in newborn cardiac defects, because it turned out this infant had a major problem with his heart. I was grateful my prayer had been heard and the doctor was right outside the door so that we could get this baby the attention he needed without any unnecessary delays.

"Baby John" encountered many challenges during his stay in the NICU. The physicians, nurses, respiratory therapists, pharmacists, surgeons, social workers, physical and occupational therapists, nutritionists, and clerical staff all watched as his little body struggled to live. It was an effort for him just to breathe. We thought we'd lost him many times, but he continued to fight for his life. I was one of the nurses recruited to take care of John on a regular basis. As nurses, we work eight-hour shifts so there were three nurses per day taking care of him. We tried to be as consistent as possible with him so he could develop a routine with the nursing staff and with his parents. By establishing a routine and consistent care, it was easier for him to progress with his developmental milestones like smiling, turning over, grasping for objects, and so forth. The home environment allows for playtime, quiet time, and provides a sense of day and night.

When an infant is in the hospital, it is a challenge to create a home-like environment; so in addition to all of the tubes and other medical equipment, his crib had toys and a mobile. One day I came to work to care for John. He was lying on his back in his crib with his ventilator tubing attached to his tracheostomy. A tracheostomy is an artificial airway which is surgically inserted through the windpipe to allow him to breathe. I got settled, said hello to him, and immediately wound up his musical mobile. John gave me the biggest smile, which warmed my heart. This was the first time I had seen him smile. I always talked to him, but had not seen him smile. I brought everyone over to see him smile and told his parents when they called that their son had a big surprise for them. They were elated when they saw him smile.

He soon started to wave his hands towards his mobile and became very interactive with staff. From that point on there was one rule that all three of his nurses agreed on: if anyone had to check something at his bedside, like charts, monitors, his IVs, medications, or examine him, they would have to wind his mobile and play with him. This included everyone from the physician to the person who just checked a chart. Soon everyone wanted to say hi and stop by to play with him.

During the five months he was in the NICU, the staff developed a strong bond with John. He connected with everyone who entered the unit, especially the staff. He was actually nurturing us! If it was a difficult day in the unit, someone would go by and say hi to John, and you could see the smile on the person's face as they played with him. John was truly an angelic gift to the NICU staff. At five months old, he went home on his ventilator with all his toys, smiling. The newborn intensive care is a busy, somewhat stressful place to work, and this "little angel" melted our hearts and brought us together as a staff. Our day would start off with our favorite topic: "What's little John up to today?"

Angels come to us in a variety of ways, and some of them come to us in human form. Little John came into this life and touched everyone who met him. It was obvious that this precious newborn was an angelic gift to those of us honored to meet him and care for him. He touched everyone who came into contact with him, and they felt joyful for the contact. This little angel was a precious gift that was given to us in the NICU to remind us of how important it is to be open to receiving love. He had enough love for all of us.

Birth Coaching with the Angels

As an RN, I also work with parents in other ways at the hospital. I assist parents as a birth coach and advocate during deliveries. My role as a birth coach began when friends asked me to attend their deliveries and help coach them through their birthing process. Friends then referred others they knew who were having babies and whom they felt could benefit from my services. This is how my work as a birth coach evolved. I love assisting parents through their birth experience; it is an honor and very different than being the official nurse attending the delivery. There are many birthing stories, and each experience is amazing and unique.

This story is about working as a birth coach with one particular couple and what happened during that process. I was referred to a couple who was interviewing doulas to assist them in the birth of their baby. A doula is someone who helps the mother during labor, providing emotional support and assistance before, during, and after the birth, as well as ensuring that both parents are included in this process. After an interview, I was hired; I met with the parents throughout the pregnancy, which progressed normally and without complication. As it got closer to the delivery date, I asked to meet with the prospective parents to review some details about what their preferences were before, during, and after the birth. The parents and I had covered this information previously. However, I felt it would be beneficial to all to review the information they had given me, as it was three weeks prior to the mother's due date.

The day I was to meet with the mother, I heard an angelic voice that gave me detailed instructions about how the delivery would progress. I was told not to be alarmed that she—referring to the baby—would be small; the baby would be healthy. This voice also told me that the mother does not want to have medication, but there would be a point where she would change her mind. I was told to support her decision about this, as it would help her rest and then she would be prepared for the remaining six hours before the baby was born. The voice told me that there would be many angels in the room and that mom would begin chanting with her breathing. I was told that mom would begin chanting when she was holding our hands—her husband's and mine. This would fill the room with light and ease the tension of the medical staff that was present. There would be a point prior to the chanting when a cesarean section would be recommended, but it would not be necessary.

The message I was receiving was so detailed that I decided to write it down. Towards the end of the message, a very wise voice introduced herself as the little girl that was going to be born. The parents did not know the sex of the infant. She gave specific details about what her mother was doing the previous day and said how much she loved to hear her mother laugh. She said that she loved her parents very much and was excited to be with them. She also said that she was coming early and not to worry because she was healthy and fine. There was a giggle and then the message ended. I did not know if I would share any of this information with the mother at our next meeting.

I met with the mother later that day and we reviewed the details of her birth plan, where to meet, we confirmed telephone numbers and so forth. Then I told the mother that I received some information about her delivery and that everything was going to be fine. I asked if she wanted to hear more about the information I received. The mother was very excited and open to hearing it, so I shared most of the information with her, including the sex of the infant. The mother said she had a dream that she was going to have a baby girl. I told her what the little girl said about what the mother was doing the day before and about her laugh. She was surprised with this information and validated the details that were given.

The next day, I received an early phone call from the father saying that they were on their way to the hospital, that labor had begun. The baby was about to be born, three weeks early. Every detail the angelic voice had given me the day before was playing out step by step. The mother decided to take some medication to rest. The obstetrician came in stated that a cesarean section was necessary and said they were preparing the room. The mother asked for her husband's hand and my hand, and started chanting as she breathed. A peaceful calm settled in the room, and the obstetrician and nurses were no longer rushing around. The chanting went on for some time, and I could feel the presence of angels in the room. The monitor strip, which records the mother's contractions and the infant's heart rate looked normal, so they no longer considered doing a cesarean section. Six hours after the mother had her medication and rested, a beautiful baby girl was born.

The newborn intensive care team entered to examine the infant and to make a decision whether or not to admit her into NICU. The delivery took place at a hospital I had worked at over twenty years ago. I recognized the newborn intensive care physician and nurse, and they remembered me. I examined the infant with them, and the physician and nurse asked what I thought about admitting the infant to newborn intensive care for observation. I replied that she was beautiful, healthy, with stable breathing and heart rate, and I didn't think that it would be necessary. They agreed, and the baby immediately went back to her mother and began breastfeeding. The baby was small and healthy, precisely as the angelic voice said. The baby did well and was able to go home with her parents. The angels surrounded this beautiful family and participated in this angelically guided birth.

Every blade of grass has its angel

that leans over it and whispers,

"Grow, grow."

---The Talmud

TERI HUNTER
LAGUNA BEACH, CA

Teri Hunter is a psychic-medium, ANGEL THERAPY PRACTIONER®, Reiki Master, and life coach with over twenty-five years of experience. She has studied various teachings and philosophies, taking bits and pieces of each to form her own unique viewpoint. Some of her favorite teachers include Marianne Williamson, Michael Bernard Beckwith, James Ray Vaughn, John Edward, Caroline Myss, Wayne Dyer, and Doreen Virtue.

She is currently coordinating small groups focused on studying the concepts and implementation of the Laws of Attraction. "I find people are my best teachers. Our diversity, our viewpoints, and our actions always teach me something new about myself. It is with immense gratitude I offer my service to others," she says. For more information or a reading, you may contact Teri at www.terihunter.com.

Down is Up!

By Teri Hunter

It was the summer of 2003 and I had just moved home to Orange County, California, from North Carolina. Over the last few years I'd seen too much radical change, and my soul craved some sense of normalcy. On a blisteringly hot August morning, my cell phone rang. It never occurred to me this could be a defining moment. Today, I look back on the events that led up to that moment and I realize I had been waiting for that phone to ring all along. There I was, forty-three years old, and I had completely lost my way. Everything I knew about myself and my life was changing. Up was down and down was up. I had unsuccessfully changed careers and thrown myself into peril, financially—as if I had been in good financial shape to begin with. I had impulsively moved across the country in a futile attempt to leave all my failed dreams and relationships behind.

Now I was living with Sweet Annie—my brother-in-law's mother—crammed into the spare bedroom of her Southern

California apartment with my two cats, their litter box poised beside my bed. Annie was desperately afraid of cats and graciously offered to put her fears aside to help me come home, but the cats had to remain locked in the bedroom. My sense of self was plummeting at an alarming rate.

I had taken a job managing a small Newport Beach bakery. I was behind the bakery, dumping the trash, when my cell phone rang.

"Ms. Hunter, we regret to inform you the moving van carrying your property to California has been stolen. The containers holding your possessions were burned in the Mojave Desert. There is no chance for recovery. We will provide you a copy of the police report and suggest you contact your insurance company as soon as possible."

It was one of those Alice-in-Wonderland moments, where everything was suddenly distorted and I felt as though I had been tossed down the rabbit's hole. I couldn't move. The world was swirling around me.

I don't know how much time went by before one of the bakery employees came looking for me. The minute she touched my shoulder I felt myself lurch back into my body. I started to cry. Everything in my life was gone, as if I never existed. The bakery sent me home. But I didn't have a home, not one I could call my own. I felt myself falling farther into a place I couldn't afford to go. You know—that place inside you that's so dark you may never find your way out. I needed light. I needed to feel the sun.

I went to a nature reserve called the Back Bay. I walked and walked. *Move forward,* I told myself. I thought if my legs stopped moving, my head would explode off my shoulders. This was all so surreal. Could it really be happening? I did a mental inventory of all the things that meant so much to me. My grandmother's wedding photo, my pictures, all of my grandfather's letters, his sweater; the one he wore every day—gone! That sweater had his scent. When I wore it I could feel him with me. I kept telling myself, *Keep moving, first one foot, then the other.*

I cried to Heaven, "I need that sweater now more than ever. All I want to do is to put it on and feel safe and protected." I knew, in that moment, that *I* had to make myself feel safe and protected. I walked faster; I cried unabashedly. Suddenly, I had the strangest feeling of familiarity. I had cried all day, but now those tears were replaced with a sense of knowing: this situation was fated. Somehow I had agreed to have this experience. I felt responsible for it, and in taking that responsibility, an opportunity existed. But what was the opportunity? And why did I have to work so hard to find it?

My brain felt like a yo-yo bouncing between wanting to play the victim and knowing a higher purpose was to be revealed. I replayed the move in my head. When I went to North Carolina, I had meticulously packed my things, labeled boxes, created an inventory sheet broken down room by room. I rented a moving van and drove across the country. For the move home, I threw things in boxes as if the house were on fire.

The day the moving men were supposed to come, they were delayed and showed up sixteen hours late. My inner voice was screaming at me, *Look at these guys!* They didn't have the proper dolly or packing materials, and the head guy looked like he was going to have a heart attack as he lugged my furniture, cigarette dangling from his lips, down the stairs and into the truck. With each trip up and down, his face grew paler and my sense of dread grew stronger. I honestly felt my back against the wall. How could I explain and justify to my family changing plane tickets, rescheduling the move, and inconveniencing everyone because I had a "feeling?" Frankly, I didn't have the money to trust my "feelings." I had already borrowed from everyone I knew to make the move home. It was almost as if I would rather lose everything than to have everyone think I was a whack job. I could hear them: "Oh, Teri had another one of her *feelings*."

Thoughts raced through my head: *If I stop everything now, nothing bad will happen, so there will be no evidence that I was right. They will all think I've gone over the edge.* As the doors of the moving van closed for the last time, I turned, looked at my sister and said, "It will be a miracle if I ever see these things again." She just stared at me with one of those *Are you crazy?* looks only a sister can give you.

Now everything was gone, really truly gone. The reality would hit me in tidal waves. One evening I sat on Annie's patio with a glass of wine and a notebook. I was struggling with another round of "Inventory Your Life," a game show hosted by my insurance company. I became increasingly depressed as I mentally walked through my kitchen, seeing all my beautiful cookware I had spent years collecting, remembering parties I hosted, friends, food, and laughter. With tears streaming down my face, my hand unconsciously started to move the pen across the page.

The power you seek, the power to change your life, to rise above your circumstances, is inside you now. It is not hidden or locked away. It is power you use every day without realizing. The power you seek is the power you reject. The power to manifest lies inside the pattern in which you speak to yourself, what you believe about yourself, in how you have defined yourself. When how you have defined yourself no longer serves you—redefine! So much of human struggle comes from one's refusal to redefine.

To redefine, change your inner dialogue; simply state that which you seek with gratitude, and so it is! To be specific, you have created affirmations to bring forth that which you desire. Yet you have been affirming lack of what you desire within your inner dialogue. Unconsciously you decide "I can't, I am not, I don't" as real and true. It is simply your inner dialogue creating your experience—redefine! Affirm "I can, I am, I do." It is that simple. There is no need to spend money or look for outside tools to change what no longer serves you.

The power of the words following "I am, I can, I do" are the seeds of manifestation. As you go through your day hear the words you say after "I am." Do they serve your greatest desires or do they lock you in the place you are? One obvious way to determine this is in your comfort level. Are you comfortable affirming "I am not"? Does it feel familiar, like an old slipper? Now affirm "I am." I am enjoying romantic love. I am enjoying wealth beyond my wildest imagination. I am loved unconditionally. I am beautiful. Are you comfortable with this inner dialogue or does it feel uncomfortable? If you seek to be comfortable embrace that which makes you uncomfortable, in doing so you shall manifest your comfort. And so it is!!

When my hand stopped moving, I read what was written. Everything made sense, sort of!

The most joyous aspect of the bakery was its customers; each person a colorful character with his or her special affection for the place. I had grown to love them all, and enjoyed chatting with them and getting to know their families. Word of my loss spread quickly, some of regulars had seen me leave the restaurant in tears the day I found out. I hadn't considered my job at the bakery could be gift from the Divine, but it was. People started bringing me things they thought I might need. Some brought me gifts to lift my spirits. The practical folks brought sheets and towels. Some of these people I knew well; others, not at all. Strangers would stop me and say they were inspired by me. They couldn't understand how I got up in the morning. I told them the outpouring of love gave me hope and reason. Through the kindness of strangers, I could feel myself engulfed by the wings of angels. I felt the angels smile as my heart opened in recognition. For the first time, I saw myself for who I really was: I am not my job, or my income, or my circumstances... I am my *love*. I heard the angels say "You *are* greatly loved, Sweet Child. All you ever need or have ever needed, you possess right now. Your loving heart inspires others." Tears fell, this time for a completely different reason.

Life had become a blur of bureaucratic red tape. I felt like two people were living inside me. One half of me wanted to throw myself on the ground, kicking and screaming, "Someone take care of this for me!" The other half reminded me that I'd created this experience. During this crisis I had, for the most part, chosen my reactions. I was learning that I get to choose how I define myself and my situations. I could buy into the general consensus of how I was "supposed" to feel, or I could *choose* how I felt. In conscious choice, I found my power.

There were days when the push and pull of not truly being able to mourn the loss of my stuff was driving me nuts. I wanted so much to have a major pity party; the trouble was, I couldn't pity myself long enough to get the ice cream out of the freezer. Living in the bedroom with the cats had become unbearably confined. I had so much to do and no money to do it with. I contacted the moving company, only to discover that the old adage is true: you get what you pay for. I had gone cheap, insured the load by its weight for some inane amount, like a penny a pound. Every time I called back, a different representative was assigned to my case. No one had any information. I was frustrated, tired, and feeling tremendous defeat.

My thoughts drifted to a night months earlier in North Carolina. I was sitting in the living room when my attention was drawn to the fire sprinklers lining the ceiling. I had an epiphany: *I don't have to burn down the house to have everything destroyed, my neighbors could do it.* For the first time ever, I got renter's insurance. While planning the move back to California I called the insurance company to see what would be covered. The agent told me only total devastation would be covered. I said, "Oh that won't happen."

The angels are clearly watching over me. They knew this was coming, and that nudge to get the renter's insurance was to be my saving grace. This experience had yielded another blessing: the insurance would cover most of the debt. I trusted the thought *get that insurance*, and now it was saving my behind.

Six months went by, and I started to have bouts of real anger. I was emotionally spent. Every time I thought I finished the insurance company's requirements, they'd ask for something else, which I couldn't deliver because it had been stolen. It was agonizing. I yelled at the angels— enough was enough. Instantly I felt them say, "You determine when enough is enough." They were right and I started to use that anger as a fire. I made a list, this time it was an intention list: where I wanted to live, the kind of job I wanted, the financial freedom I craved. I didn't know how the angels were going to do it, but I thanked them in advance for their help; first order of business, a place to live *sans* the bedside litter box.

I started putting the word out, telling everyone I saw I wanted to live at the beach; did they know someone with a rental? I had my enthusiasm and I trusted the angels would supply the cash. Opportunities started to manifest immediately. Within a few days, the bakery owners came to me, explaining that a long-time tenant had to move suddenly and his Laguna Beach apartment would be available after some new paint and carpet. Although it was in disarray, I could see it that afternoon.

I walked in and couldn't believe my eyes. This quaint little one-bedroom apartment had the most amazing ocean view. I was mesmerized. I could hear the waves breaking on the sand, see people playing in the white water. I could see San Clemente Island. I was elated. Ding, ding! The light bulb went off: I would *never* have fit in this tiny little place. The angels replaced my old stuff with an ocean!!! How cool is that?

The job at the bakery paid a third of what I was used to making and the hours were taking their toll. I was grateful to the owners for their help getting the apartment, knowing full well they were the angels' facilitators. The rent was steep and move-in costs were over four thousand dollars. I went out on another limb—I borrowed more money. I was so scared the day I signed that lease, financially speaking. In my mind I kept hearing, *If you let money get in the way, you'll regret it.* I calculated that if I didn't eat or drink or spend one dime, I'd make it. Oops, redefine: I get to make lots more money!!

The apartment repairs couldn't go quickly enough. Once I knew I was moving, the bedroom I'd been living in had literally become stifling. I am eternally grateful to my friend, Annie, another of God's earth angels helping me along, but it was time for me to be back on my own. Moving day finally came! It was one load: an air mattress, a beach chair, an eight-inch, black-and-white television set, a set of wine glasses, and a cork screw. Thanks to all those earth angels, I had a pot to cook in. I kept reminding myself I had a "shop-whenever-you-want, guilt-free" card for life.

Just before New Year's Day 2004, I decided to "put my order" into the angels: top of the list—a new job. I went into great detail describing the environment, how it felt getting up in the morning and going to work, how much money I'd make. Five days later, I got a phone call from an old colleague. He said he had a job I was perfect for, they were offering ten thousand dollars more a year than I was currently making, plus health benefits. And I wouldn't have to work weekends or holidays anymore. I literally jumped up and down with gratitude, thanking the angels for their rapid response time and for all the blessings yet to come.

Nine months later, I had doubled my annual income and was well on my way out of the rabbits' hole. Losing *everything* afforded me the opportunity to manifest my dreams, to finally change my inner dialogue, and open space for blessings of abundance. The angels shone their light so that I could see purpose in my work and in my life. I relish the relationships I have, and rejoice in an excitement for life. None of these experiences would have been possible without me consciously noticing what I thought about myself and choosing how I want to show up in this world. The angels tell me that we can all change our lives, our circumstances, anything we want we can have right now—REDEFINE.

The golden moments in the stream

of life rush past us and

we see nothing but sand; the angels

come to visit us, and we only know them

when they are gone.

---George Elliot

MICHELLE RHIANON FAGER
OCEAN CITY, MD

F ollowing Michelle's angel experience in 1985, she continued to encounter situations involving the spirit world until she was guided in 2004 to begin teaching others about angels and spiritual enlightenment. During the interim, while practicing as a lawyer, she became an avid student of *A Course in Miracles*, which led to more premonitions and seeing angels and ascended masters. In 2000, she retired from the legal profession to focus on raising her children. In 2003, after having had many psychic dreams including the incidents surrounding September 11, 2001, Michelle was led to attend ANGEL THERAPY PRACTITIONER® training and was certified by Doreen Virtue, Ph.D.

The following year, Michelle became certified as a medium through the Mediumship Mentorship Program and later trained in the Professional Spiritual Teachers' Training program. She continued her mediumship training with James Van Praagh and later completed a course of study to become an ordained ministerial counselor through Pathways of Light, a non-denominational church based upon the principals espoused in *A Course in Miracles*. At present, Michelle's spiritual journey includes teaching classes, spiritual counseling, and individual spiritual readings. She joyfully donates all proceeds of her work to charitable causes. She is particularly guided to use her gifts to assist those people who are in the process of crossing over to the other side. Her focus is on helping others realize their divine spiritual inheritance and embracing the love that is around everyone in the form of God, angels, and ascended masters.

Angels by my Side

By Rev. Michelle Rhianon Fager

"There are always two roads to take...in the end what
seems as the long way is always the journey to the
deepest desire of the soul."

W e all have our stories to tell. Each one is a masterpiece
and a miracle in itself. I have learned that in this life,
there are no accidents; whether we are aware of it or not, we are
all guided by the hand of our Divine Creator, always and in all
ways. We are all here to learn in this journey we call life. Some of
us learn our lessons early on; some of us learn later in life. For
me, those lessons began immediately.

My birthmother's pregnancy with me was what this world would call a grievous accident. Her unmarried older sister had just had a daughter, and their mother was raising that child. Not wanting to add to her mother's burden, my birthmother bravely decided to have me on her own, vowing to disclose this secret to no one. Living in Colorado at the time, she got a map of the United States, closed her eyes, and touched her finger to the map. She opened her eyes and, removing her finger, saw the city of Syracuse, New York. Within days, she was boarding a train heading for Syracuse. In 1964, there was tremendous social stigma surrounding unwed mothers, and a general lack of support from family and society. And as many young pregnant girls chose to do, my mother surrendered me for adoption, three days following my birth, on Halloween.

I grew up in my adoptive family an extremely sensitive, inquisitive, and independent girl, quite different from their quiet, "follow the status quo and don't ask questions" nature. Being adopted, I felt very different from the other children in my neighborhood, not only in the fact that my parents were not my "real" parents, but in other ways as well. Nature fascinated me, and I remember spending days looking at trees, flowers, and plants, and intuiting their feelings about existence. As I did this, many of the emotions that I felt would shock and perplex me— where did they come from?

One time, when I was about seven years old, I received a very strong sense of Jesus around me; although I did not see an image of him, I knew he was there. A feeling of intense love overtook me, and he conveyed to me through a voice in my mind that God was my real Father. He also told me that I had been in existence for longer than seven years—in fact, for eternity—and that there was a Divine purpose for me being here, although I didn't know what that was yet. The love that emanated from Jesus brought me to tears, just as it does today when I invoke his presence and send him love.

As I grew up, I witnessed the passing of several loved ones. When I was seven, my grandmother, Marie, died of lung cancer. She spent the last few months of her life with my family at home. About a year later, my grandfather on my father's side died following a short illness. During that time period, I also lost my older cousin in a car crash. She was twenty-one. It was hard to make sense of death. None of my friends had ever lost anyone close to them.

My mother instructed me to pray for all these souls who had died every night so they would go to Heaven. I would spend evenings lying in bed reciting the Lord's Prayer and Hail Marys for these relatives, hoping I was doing some good. Yet at the same time, my prayers felt useless. As my mind would mechanically recite the prayers, I would close my eyes and watch colors moving like a kaleidoscope in my inner vision. The colors would spin into different shapes and forms, and would then materialize into people—eyes, hair, or a vague body would take shape first, and then the image would clarify and become someone I knew who had died. I knew these souls were already in Heaven, for although they never verbally communicated with me, I felt a sense of deep peace from them, and I felt comforted. I mentioned my visions to my mother once, and she reacted in such a negative way that I never mentioned them to anyone again.

Then, when I was fifteen, my mother died of lung cancer. I would venture to say that I knew intuitively that she was going to die about a year before it happened. My family never told me; in fact, they hid the severity of her condition from my sister and me right up until the end. I was thankful that I knew—it was a blessing, as it gave me time to prepare. I knew this was a major turning point in my life. From there on out, it was me against the world; I was determined to survive and do something magnificent.

It was at this point that I lost my former connections with Heaven. No longer did I have the luxury of closing my eyes and becoming lost in my imagination and visions. I knew I had Jesus and my guardian angels with me, but I did not have the full faith in them to help me survive. I was going to have to do that myself. Prior to her death, my mother was the stabilizing force in our family. She was the mother who attended every PTA meeting, school event, and dance recital. She was always at home for us with cookies, helping with homework, and in every way taking care of our existence.

Now that she was gone and my father was still working full time, I spent my high school years juggling my school work, cheerleading, drama, choir, and a part-time job, not to mention the time I had to invest doing housework and cooking for the family. I managed to keep my grades up and won a partial scholarship for college which I could use, provided I attended college in New York state. I chose Syracuse University, as it was a big school—much different from the small town I had grown up in. I thought I would like it.

The enormity and diversity of the university overwhelmed me. It was also a struggle for my father, financially. I worked almost constantly to earn spending money, unlike many of my friends, who had the luxury of having a car on campus and a monthly check sent to them. Following my first year, I returned home for the summer and became entangled with a local boy from a middle-class family similar to mine. He was less intimidating to me than the boys from college who came from a different economic background. We dated through the summer and into the next fall.

That Christmas break, I was home, attending a Christmas party with him. Everyone was celebrating the engagement of his cousin, who was a few years older than us. I distinctly remember his mother saying that this was going to be me next year. Then his father asked me why I was going to a private college when I wouldn't be doing anything, really, other than getting married. I was shocked. I made up my mind that I would never be trapped in that town or in a life like that.

More determined than ever to leave the area, I finally convinced my father a year and a half later to allow me to go to Ocean City, Maryland, with some friends from school so that I could work. I convinced him I could make loads of money, since there were plenty of summer jobs there. I remember driving to Ocean City with some girl I had just met. The other friends who were supposed to go bailed out. We drove four hundred miles in about six hours and got into town early in the morning.

I had one bag of clothes, twenty dollars, and tentative plans to rent an apartment there. My father had loaned me money as a down payment for my share of the apartment, but I needed roommates to take the places of the girls who didn't come. After staying in various apartments and beach shacks, we did finally find roommates who ended up moving in, bringing with them a few other people. The place was constantly swarming with guests and in constant disarray. I spent most of my time working as a hostess and scraping paint off condos during the day, then going to the beach and attending parties at night.

Between the rent, food, and a new wardrobe, I had little money saved; still, I decided to return home in late June for my sister's high school graduation. I got airline tickets to fly out of Salisbury and then to Baltimore-Washington International Airport on People's Express. It was cheaper than renting a car, and in any case, I didn't have a credit card, so I *couldn't* rent a car. My "friends" at the apartment drove me to the airport and promised to pick me up upon my return three days later.

After a fairly uneventful visit home, I boarded my plane. When we landed in Baltimore, I just knew something was amiss. I caught my flight to Salisbury and waited for over an hour in the Salisbury airport for my "friends" before finally realizing they were not going to show. I remember having just two dollars in my handbag. I was waiting for paychecks and was living from week to week on what I made. Thoughts spun through my mind.

What was I going to do? The only thing I could come up with was hitchhike, but I was scared of getting hurt, raped, or murdered. Already I had been approached by some less-than-savory characters during my short stay in Ocean City. I had always managed to get away from those types but didn't know what I would do if I was trapped in a car with someone like that. I couldn't walk—it was thirty miles of desolate, flat land. I would get hungry and tired before then. I couldn't call anyone. All the people I knew were only there for the summer, they didn't have telephones, and in 1985, cell phones were non-existent. I was out of options and cursing myself for not having saved more money to bring with me. I sat on one of the benches in the small airport and sobbed. "I need some help," I pleaded to God. "I don't know what to do."

Just then, a woman approached me. She looked about fifty years old, pleasantly plump with silvery blond hair. She smiled a sweet smile and gently asked me what was wrong. Reluctantly, I looked up and began telling her my plight as simply as possible. She looked at me compassionately and reached into her bag. "Here," she said, "this is for you." She drew out thirty dollars from her bag and handed it to me.

"But I can't take this from you," I said, thinking I didn't deserve this gift.

"I want you to have it," she insisted. "You can use it for bus fare to get home."

I stared at her and said, "I'm getting a paycheck when I get back. Please let me take your address, and I will mail you the money next week." I looked down at my handbag, wondering if I had a pen and some paper. She spoke quietly and laid the money gently on the bench. "Just do it for somebody else someday," she said. The words resonated with something in my heart, and I turned my eyes up to look at her. She was gone. I got up and searched the tiny airport. I looked all around the room, the ticket counter, the bathroom, outside, and all around the area.

There was no way she could have disappeared in those few seconds. I realized I was not going to find her and simply thanked God for the money. Now I could get back to my apartment. Everything felt so surreal. It was almost like I was in another time or place. Looking back, I find it hard to remember what happened next. I know I got back to Ocean City, but the details of the journey are erased from my mind.

At the time, I did not know angels could exist in human form. I know now that when any of us of need help and ask for it, our angels will come in whatever form necessary to assist us. They always come as an answer to our prayers. Sometimes it is immediate and the answer is given almost upon the asking, but most times it comes as Divine guidance, as I was to learn later.

Although the angel experience never left me and the words she spoke hung over me like a premonition, I was still in survival mode. I couldn't imagine having the ability to help someone as this angel did for me. I pushed myself onto what I believed was the road to success. I graduated college, went on to law school, got an MBA, and worked as an associate lawyer; then I opened a law practice of my own. All the while, I struggled with finances and relationships. A few years later, I began having dreams where I would see things as they were happening or about to happen on the earth. I knew there was some significance to this, but I didn't know what. It was around this time I was given a book which led me to another manuscript, entitled *A Course in Miracles*.

As soon as I began reading it, I had a profound shift in my attitude of struggle, survival, and acquisition. Instead of focusing on these things, I began a practice of gratitude. By marking each day as a blessing and remembering all the profound abundance in my life, everything began to change. My business grew and prospered as circumstances brought me wonderful clients who paid their bills on time and valued my work. I purchased my house and then my office within a short period of time after I began the practice of being grateful. I had always wanted to be a mother, and soon after this shift, I was miraculously bestowed with the gift of my son, Chase.

Later, I met my compassionate, spiritual, devoted husband, John, who blessed me with two more sons, Jack and Thomas, and shares my journey on a path of enlightenment. I have since been reunited with my birth mother who, following my birth, married a caring, wonderful man. They have since moved to the east coast, sharing their lives with us as caring, joy-filled parents and grandparents. I am continually blessed with laughter, love, and light from my beautiful girlfriends. We share together the little ups and downs of each of our unique journeys and offer support, love, and confidence to each other every day.

The spiritual gifts I left behind as a child have returned. I have been guided to teachers who have helped me understand about clairvoyance, clairsentience, and the ability we all have to connect with the angels, our deceased loved ones, and the Divine realms of existence. I am now able to empower others through spiritual readings, workshops, and spiritual counseling as a non-denominational minister. Best of all, I am able to donate every bit of the proceeds of my work to help people, animals, and environmental causes as I am Divinely guided. The angel who propelled me toward a spiritual life spoke the words that so profoundly affect my life today: "Just do it for someone else someday." Just as she reveled in the joy of service toward me, my joy now lies in giving to others and receiving the gift of Divine abundance. This abundance prevails as I continue a practice of mindful gratitude every day. I know that God, my angels, Jesus, and other ascended masters have provided—and continue to provide—the people, books, and situations I need, bestowing me with the necessary knowledge to accomplish my Divine life purpose.

Each and every one of us is a gift to the world in the mind of God. We are all here to do magnificent work in joy for ourselves and in service to others. We are all empowered with God's love, grace, and Divinity every day. It is in connecting with our Creator's Universal principles that we find our peace and our place here on earth. For me, it was the lesson of gratitude for everything I already had. We are each presented with lessons in our life journey. It doesn't matter what the lessons are, or whether we perceive our lessons as more or less difficult than anyone else's. Our soul knows what lessons are needed to learn to grow closer to God. The opportunity for a life filled with love is available to us all as Divine children of our Creator. God truly desires that we be happy. Look deeply at your own journey. There have been no mistakes. The lessons and the answers are there. You can chose to blindly follow the world's teaching of fear and lack, or you can accept and follow the love-filled guidance from God and your angels. For me, it is a journey of happiness when I feel at one with God and the angelic energy surrounding me constantly. I am "taking the long way around," and it truly is a magical journey.

Be an angel to someone else

whenever you can,

as a way of thanking God

for the help your angel has given you.

~ Eileen Elias Freeman,

The Angels' Little Instruction Book

KAREN L. BIANCO
CHERRY HILL, NJ

Karen L. Bianco lives with her husband and three children in New Jersey. She earned her certification in massage from Lourdes Institute of Wholistic Studies and her associate's degree in applied science from Camden County College in the spring of 2004.

After graduation, Karen began training in the Bach® Flower Essences. Karen now also works as a Bach Flower consultant, incorporating the healing power of the flower essences into her practice. In September of 2006, Karen became an ANGEL THERAPY PRACTITIONER®, certified by Dr. Doreen Virtue. As an ANGEL THERAPY PRACTITIONER®, Karen also incorporates angel readings and healings into her practice, Angel Essence Massage.

Karen's website is www.angelesencemassage.com and her email is Karen@angelessencemassage.com. She can also be reached by calling (856) 207-7282.

Making The Connection

By Karen L. Bianco

I guess I was always a weird kid. Up until I was nine or ten, I was frequently visited during the night by a mysterious "woman" that no one else could see or hear—Mother Mary. I was profoundly psychic, frequently making predictions that would later come true. I was also hyper and never shut up, always asking questions about everything. My folks hoped I would grow out of my oddities, but it was not to be—instead of growing out of them, I seemed to grow into them. Fortunately, I wasn't the only "weird" one in my family. My sister and I share a strong connection with each other and the world around us.

Our family has a rich spiritual heritage. I am the baby, with two older sisters. My mother is half Irish, half Italian, one hundred percent Catholic. My father is a southern boy of Cherokee, Creeke, and English descent, whose quiet style is a perfect match for my mother's take-charge personality. I have always felt proud of my Native American blood, feeling deeply connected to Native American traditions and people. I remember playing with little cowboy and Indian figurines, and the Indians were the good guys. After all, they were the ones who picked up their trash!

My maternal grandmother was a little Italian woman with a heart of gold. An avid gardener with a passion for serving dandelion green salads, she simply loved to have her hands in the dirt. She also happened to talk to Jesus like he was a guest sitting on her plastic-covered sofa. Grandmom talked to him constantly. If one of us stubbed our toe, she called on him to take away the pain. To find a misplaced paper, she asked him to send Saint Anthony to help. She never doubted he was there, listening. I am blessed that she gave me such an amazing introduction to connecting with Spirit.

When I was in the first grade, I brought my favorite book to school for the teacher to read to the class. Unfortunately, she wasn't allowed to read it—the book was about Jesus, and I attended a public school. I was devastated and went home, crying. I had to go to school every day! I didn't want to go to a place where Jesus wasn't welcome! My parents decided that I would start attending our parish Catholic school the next year. Even in a Catholic school, where we spoke of God and the saints on a daily basis, I did not feel safe enough to speak freely of my almost nightly encounters with Spirit.

I was desperately afraid of the dark. I remember sitting on my bed with my blankets pulled over my head, too afraid to peek out, saying the Hail Mary over and over again. I was calling Mary to me with those prayers, and as a child, I did not question if it was real when I saw her—I was just happy to not be alone in the dark anymore. Initially, I wasn't sure who my comforting nighttime visitor was—when I told my family about her, I referred to her as "the lady in blue." The mystery lady was identified one day when I was in preschool, though, when I saw a painting of the Virgin Mary. My mother remembers me exclaiming, "That's the lady who visits me!"

Sometimes Mother Mary and I would talk about the people around me, sometimes she would give me messages for them; most of the time, though, she just comforted me until I went back to sleep.

My mom told me that the Blessed Mother Mary loves all children and that she probably had a special spot in her heart for sick children, like me. I was suffering from night terrors and chronic severe urinary track infections. I was seeing specialists for the urinary issues, and I even had my urethra dilated a couple of times. The specialist I was seeing at Children's Hospital in Philadelphia, Pennsylvania, wanted to perform an invasive test on me to determine exactly what was causing my problem, but my family doctor warned my parents that the test could cause psychological damage.

The night before the test, as my mother prayed to God for my health, she began to feel guilty. She wondered, *How can I ask*

God to heal my daughter's body when I am polluting my own body by smoking cigarettes? She told God she would not smoke another cigarette and asked Him to heal me. She told God she knew He could do it, if it was His will. My mother then called the doctor the next day and cancelled the test. I honestly believe my mother's plea to God helped heal me, along with another event—a hands-on healing that occurred at my grandparents' home. Grandmom had my sisters and me hold hands. She prayed out loud to Jesus, Mother Mary, our Father in Heaven, and the Holy Sprit as she laid her hands on my abdomen. All of a sudden I felt something move under her hands; she felt it, too. Miraculously, I was healed! I did go back to the urologist several times after that, only for follow-up visits and urinalysis. I never got another urinary tract infection. The doctor said there was no explanation for why they just stopped, but we knew—*God's love had healed me!*

While my parents were pleased and grateful for my physical healing, there was another etheric phenomenon that they weren't nearly as open to: my budding psychic abilities. I was in middle school when my mother was driving past a carnival set up at the local high school. I pointed out the Ferris wheel and said, "Next time they use that, it's going to break." The next day we found out my cousins, Anthony and Frankie, were at the carnival when the Ferris wheel malfunctioned and people were stuck in the cars. It wouldn't have been a serious problem, but someone panicked and either fell from their car or jumped.

When I heard about it, I remember thinking, *How did I know that? Why did I know that?* According to everything I learned in church, fortune telling was taboo. Since I was predicting the future, was I bad? *Why can't I just know the answers in math class?* I lamented. *Why do I have to be so weird?*

Part of me, however, acknowledged that the information that I received *was correct.* I had no idea what was going on, what was causing these psychic episodes. I was filled with questions. My mother didn't make a big deal about it when these things happened—I think my psychic abilities frightened her. I sensed that she didn't like to talk about it. Her response simply made me further question if I was doing something wrong.

By the time I was in high school, my psychic "hits" were coming more frequently. I would just "know" things before they would happen. Sometimes, out of the blue, a little movie would play out in my mind, as if I was remembering something that had already happened. The weird thing was it *hadn't* happened yet. The thought would just pop in, uninvited!

My psychic abilities sometimes even enabled me to communicate with the deceased. When I was sixteen, on the morning of the one-year anniversary of the death of my paternal grandmother, Mamaw. I was in the bathroom putting on makeup and getting ready for school. Then I heard a thud in the living room. No one else was awake. I walked into the room and saw Mamaw's picture had fallen to the floor. As I replaced it, I *knew* Mamaw was letting me know that she was still watching over us. I didn't see her or hear her speak. I just *knew.* I also felt her presence—her playful, sweet energy. I accepted it casually, confidentially, just as if she had called on the phone to say, "Hi!"

By the time I was a young woman, I was learning to let my psychic nudges work for me. One day, I was making dinner—I had mixed the ingredients for meatballs and shaped them—but just as I was about to start frying them, I stopped. In that moment, I *knew* that my boyfriend was going to call me for a ride home. I sat down at my kitchen table and waited for the phone call. He was out with the guys and he had never before asked me to come get him when he was out with his friends. Nonetheless, I knew he would, and I didn't want to have to leave half-cooked meatballs in the frying pan. I felt silly, but I followed my instincts, and he called a few minutes later. I answered the phone, saying, "You need me to pick you up, don't you?" This event really cemented in me the importance of paying attention to my intuitive feelings. I had finally grown up and learned to accept my intuition.

Even as I learned to accept my inner knowing, my psychic abilities were expanding. When I was in my early twenties, I shared a profound experience with my sister, Madeline. In some ways, I think it was a turning point for us both, propelling us both forward on our spiritual quests. Madeline was watching my daughter Tammie for me when I worked. One morning I arrived at my sister's to find a note on the storm door. She had left the door unlocked, and the note said she needed to stop at the cleaners and the supermarket. I carried Tammie into the house and put her down on the kitchen floor, still in the car seat.

She stretched and called out for her "baba," so I unhooked the buckle in the car seat and handed her the bottle. I expected her to happily suck her bottle for the thirty seconds it would take me to duck outside to get her baby bag. Tammie had different ideas; she was just getting ready to walk, and she would crawl around and pull herself up on furniture or people. She crawled over to the door and pushed it shut, locking herself in the house alone. Immediately I worried that she would make her way to the other side of the kitchen and try to pull herself up on the door that led to the basement. If she fell, the steep steps and concrete floor would kill her.

I yelled through the door, "Look at Mommy, Tammie, look at Mommy!" I was panicking. She wasn't interested in what I was saying at all. I wondered if I should break the kitchen window to get to her—but what if the flying glass hurt her? The best thing that could possibly happen in that moment was for my sister to come home with her keys and unlock the door. I shouted, "Madeline, don't go to the supermarket! Come right home!" I shouted those exact words, with my fists clenched, stomping my foot. Then I called to Tammie again, trying to keep her attention on me.

All of a sudden, my sister's car flew into her driveway. She put the car in park, back tires throwing rocks behind them as she leapt from the car with it still running. "I heard you say, 'Madeline, don't go to the supermarket! Come right home!'" she was yelling as she ran towards me.

"Hurry, hurry!" was all I could say.

Once we were inside and Tammie was safe, we looked at each other, a little spooked and very excited. What had just happened? How did we do that? We had covered new territory in our psychic adventures.

Around the same time, we saw a special on television about the work of Edgar Cayce. Cayce is sometimes referred to as "The Sleeping Prophet." His work examined many of the mysteries that intrigued both me and Madeline. Cayce's work felt authentic from the start. The Association for Research and Enlightenment, or A.R.E., is dedicated to preserving and studying Cayce's work, as well as getting the word out to others. Dreams were one of the subjects that Cayce explored in his readings that first intrigued us. I've always had vivid dreams—sometimes the dreams are great, but sometimes they are super scary. I have also dreamt of people's faces before I met them or dreamt of a moment in time that later passes.

Madeline often dreams of family and friends. She sees them exactly as they look in their caskets, months before their death. Grandmom once came to her in a dream with a warning that Madeline needed to get up because her father had just suffered a stroke. Madeline called my mom first thing in the morning and told her about the dream, wanting my dad to go for a check up. Dad got home from work and my mom told him about the dream—he brushed it off. Just then, he began to have a violent seizure. The ambulance came and brought him to the hospital. My father wound up with a couple of broken ribs from the seizure, and the doctors said that he had meningitis. The fact that it turned out to be meningitis and not a stroke was not as significant as the warning itself—I believe that my grandmother was trying to prepare us that my father was going to face a health crisis, which left him with permanent damage. She was always looking over Daddy during his long recovery.

Cayce encouraged keeping a dream journal, and my sister and I began to follow his advice. With practice and patience, it became easier to recall my dreams and interpret the messages they sometimes held. My interest lead me to purchase the book, *Our Dreaming Mind*, by Robert L. Van De Castle, Ph.D. I was amazed at how many people used dream time to solve problems when solutions eluded them in their waking hours. The book is packed full of information about dreams, including giving many examples of how dreams have had a positive impact on everything from art and science to medicine and sports. Seeing how others utilize this tool to improve their lives and the lives of others is truly uplifting; it also validates the importance of dream analysis. The periodic table of elements, the sewing machine, and the successful isolation of the hormone insulin are just a few of the scientific advances that were discovered using knowledge found in dreams. Many artists and writers have credited their dreams for creating inspiration and removing blocks. Salvador Dali, Orson Welles, Mary Shelley, Robert Louis Stevenson, and Charlotte Brontë are among those discussed in *Our Dreaming Mind*.

I had another profound psychic experience in 2002 when I stumbled upon the work of Dr. Edward Bach, the developer of Bach® Flower Essences. As soon as I began to read his story, the hair stood up on my entire body—head to toe—and I began to cry. Suddenly I *knew* I was meant to use the tools developed by this remarkable man in my healing practice. Reading about his work was like running into an old familiar friend, like coming home. As I continued to study herbs and their uses, it was like a light bulb went on over my head—Grandmom, with her endless dandelion green salads, must have intuitively known about this miracle plant's healing capabilities. Now I was continuing the tradition, intentionally using herbs and Bach® Flower Essences to heal others.

I had gone from conversations with an ascended master and precognition to telepathic communication and tapping into the intuitive power of my dreams. It never occurred to me, however, that I could instigate these communications with Spirit. And I had just recently realized that I could hear Heaven's messages more clearly if I pay attention and notice patterns. I started to embrace meditation, to listen to the silence within.

During my training with Doreen Virtue, I learned that you have to ask a question of Spirit and then listen for the answer—just like when you are having a conversation with someone in flesh and blood in front of you. I've found the angels to be readily available assistants, eager to deliver God's guidance directly. The trick is learning how to trust the answers we receive from them. Frequently when we don't like the answers we get, we brush them off. And then when things go wrong after we've ignored the messages from the angels or our gut, we realize "I knew it!" or "I had a feeling this would happen."

In a world so full of stimuli, it's sometimes difficult for us to hear and trust our angels as they gently nudge us along on our path in life. But as we exercise our psychic muscles, they become more noticeable. When we have the intention to hear angels, guides, or loved ones—and when we have an intention to be of service to others—we begin to hear messages clearly and easily; equally as important, we learn to trust the messages we receive.

Have joy in your heart, know that God loves you, and He is waiting patiently for you to call on either Him or one of his

All God's angels come to us

disguised.

~James Russell Lowell

PAMELA HIGA JOHNSON
HONOLULU, HAWAII

Pamela Higa Johnson has been a conscious channel since 1987 when she experienced a profound spiritual awakening that transformed her life completely and set her squarely on her life path. A gifted spiritual healer, inspirational speaker, workshop presenter, and teacher of metaphysics, Pamela is based in Hawaii on the island of Oahu. She lives with her husband, psychic medium, Alan Johnson, and their son, Taylor. Together, Pamela and Alan maintain an active client base that spans the globe.

Pamela conducts workshops, classes, special events, and telephone seminars for her clients in Hawaii, throughout the U.S., and around the world. Her current focus is to reach spiritual seekers by teaching classes over the telephone and the Internet. Visit Pamela's website at www.spiritplanet.net to be added to her newsletter and emailing list. Her mailing address is Spirit Planet, P.O. Box 688, Kaneohe, Hawaii 96744.

The Angel Channel

By Pamela Higa Johnson

What you are about to read is a unique collaboration, the result of the blending together of my consciousness with that of my spiritual team of guides and angels. I have been blessed to serve as the conscious channel for a collective group of spiritual entities, known as the High Council, for twenty years now. The High Council is comprised of various ascended masters, angels, and spiritual teachers and guides from other dimensions. They include Jesus, Archangel Michael, and Kwan Yin, among others. I refer to the entities interchangeably as my guides, or Spirit. There are times when I truly do not know where I end and they begin, so total and all-encompassing is my relationship with the High Council at this point. Along with God, these wise and loving beings continue to be my greatest teachers and loving companions in Spirit.

I define my relationship with the High Council as a sort of co-tenancy. They are an integral part of my daily life. Yes, I have free will, which means I can live my life as I choose, which I certainly do. However, I have found that when I allow God and Spirit to guide me, the rewards often surpass anything I could think of on my own. Every single blessing that I have in my life today came as a result of following their Divine guidance.

As you read on, you will notice that the guides often use the word, "you." They tell me they do this so you will know and feel that they are speaking directly to you. Make no mistake, there is powerful, loving energy being transmitted from them to you through these pages. Simply open your heart and your mind to receive.

As the guides like to say: *Let us begin....*

Q: What is channeling?

Channeling is an act of inspiration, when someone is guided by Divine influence or a higher power. A channel is someone who has learned how to set their conscious mind aside, raise their vibration, and allow a spiritual being or energy to flow through them. This is primarily done for the purpose of the channel's own spiritual growth and in some cases, to also fulfill their life purpose of guiding, healing, and teaching others. The channel becomes a human communication link and serves as a translator of sorts, acting as the channel for the messages and healing energy to come into the physical world. It is possible for anyone to channel since each of you has the potential to raise your vibration and connect with the Divine beings who share your space.

This does not mean that all channels are equal in accuracy and content. The quality of the channeled information can vary widely, depending upon the channel's own level of spiritual awareness, their natural intelligence, and their ability to achieve a state of neutrality. Remaining emotionally neutral is important so that the channel's emotions, including their own personal beliefs, issues, and preferences, do not influence or interfere with the intended message.

Therefore, we advise you to not automatically accept all channeled messages as true. Practice discernment. Learn how to perceive the energy contained in the information. You can learn how to see and feel the truth, as it has a distinct energy all of its own. God's truth touches the core of you and is unmistakable to those who are spiritually awakened. Guides will utilize everything that the channel understands and already knows to bring their message through, which may explain why the best channels are often highly intelligent, independent, and multi-faceted individuals.

Q: Who are the entities that people channel?

The entities channeled might be spirit guides, ascended masters, angels, or even galactic beings from other dimensions beyond space and time. Any of these entities can take the role of a guide. Whatever their origin, your spiritual helpers share the goal of helping you evolve with grace and joy. Your guides are always near, gently nudging you in the right direction when you are lost, doing their best to encourage you when you falter, and always helping to lead you to your highest and greatest good. When you give your consciousnes permission for them to connect with you, a Divine and loving partnership can blossom that can transform your life forever.

Almost everyone has had an experience of receiving guidance or inspiration that later proved to be accurate or even life-changing. This happens because Spirit is constantly impressing messages upon your conscious mind when you are awake. Your mind is like a radio receiver that is picking up signals continuously, even if the signals are being transmitted on a frequency that is too high for you to hear. Throughout your day, you shift back and forth through different states and levels of consciousness. This is because your consciousness is never static. Your brain waves oscillate and change frequency depending upon your emotional state and the activities in which you are engaged.

There are times when you are more relaxed and receptive, and there are other times when your worry or fear thoughts create static, making their transmissions more difficult for you to perceive. Whatever the case, your guides are there to help you and will do their best to attune to your vibration. All they ask is that you do your part and learn how to quiet your thoughts and calm your emotions. Hold this intention, and they will help you raise your vibration so they can more easily blend with your energy.

Q: Can you further explain the channeling process?

When Pamela channels, she is bathed in a sea of love and light so pure and unconditional that it lifts her spirits almost instantly. She is nourished on every level of her being as we blend with her energy. Pamela's consciousness then merges with ours and the transmissions of energy, guidance, and healing begin to flow.

When you open as a channel, your perspective on life gradually changes. Worrisome, mundane issues that have bothered you begin to lose their significance. Creative solutions start to flow spontaneously. In time, you become more accepting and forgiving of others. You feel whole and complete. In this way, learning to channel can be a spiritual rebirth that may lead to a profound healing as well as a full awakening of your spiritual power. This is available to anyone! All you need to have is a desire to make the connection with your guides. Ask and the assistance will be given. It is Universal law that what you ask for is always given to you, though it may not be in the form your conscious mind expects.

Channeling is a journey, not a destination.

Learning to channel takes commitment, persistence, and a willingness to put your ego/conscious mind aside to allow your guides and angels to speak to you. While the process is actually a simple one, the individuals who find channeling easiest to learn are often those who have already done some preliminary emotional work to heal and clear their issues and blocks. The clearer and more balanced you are emotionally, the easier it is for Spirit to communicate with you. In addition, the Law of Attraction, or "like attracts like," is always at work in your life, and so it is with channeling. You will draw to yourself an angel, spiritual entity, or ascended master, who is in harmony with your present level of spiritual awareness. This of course can, and will, change as you evolve.

Q: Can you tell me more about this Law of Attraction?

The manifestation process is very simple. You create from your thoughts and beliefs, combined with your emotions, which are then reinforced by your actions. Your belief programs are continually running in the background of your awareness and creating your reality, thus you can identify what they are by what is going on in your life right now. When your belief is combined with strong emotion (e.g. fear, joy), you will draw to yourself the energy, people, things, or experiences that match it. This is one of the basic Laws of the Universe.

You are already a master Creator! Look around you and see the life that your beliefs have created. This is true for everyone. If you do not like what you have created, you can change it!

Change your beliefs and your reality will change! It is the law.

You can have whatever you want and believe you can have. Again, you are already doing this right now. You can create what you like! Before you do, please consider this: when you raise your consciousness to connect to God the Creator, you will automatically attract the greatest good to yourself. Here is a truth that few understand—God's will is actually your authentic will! They can be one and the same. It is not about surrendering your will to a Higher Power, but about embracing your full Divine power. True spiritual power means living as your genuine God-self, not as your false ego self.

Surrendering to God's will means your will is one with His and your full spiritual power is then fully activated.

Q: What about free will and fate?

Yes, there is an element called fate at work in your reality, but it is self-created, not imposed upon you externally, and certainly not by God. For in His likeness you were created and so it is that God gives you the power to manifest what you choose. Sometimes your manifestations are beautiful and uplifting, at other times, they create disharmony and even suffering. Whatever the case, you are the master of your own small universe. In addition, when you work with the Creator by aligning your will to His will, your manifestations instantly take on a higher, more expanded quality.

When you seek to create and choose what is for the highest good of everyone, not just yourself, you are set free from the karmic cycle.

Q: What is the purpose of existence?

All of you share the same goal of learning how to live harmoni-ously. You begin by discovering what creates harmony in your life as well as what undermines it, and then you learn how to deliberately create harmony. In addition, you also have your own unique destiny path that you have chosen. It is easy to recognize when you have found your path, for you will feel either a tingle of excitement or disconcerting fear, depending upon what issues you have. Your emotions are your personal navigation system, signaling to you what is really going on within you and what you are on the verge of creating from those feelings.

Whatever you gain in understanding and wisdom in this life, you eventually contribute back to God/Source when you return home. God is love and that love is alive, which means that like God, you are constantly growing, learning, and expanding. Life always moves forward. Life does not stand still or have any real boundaries. Life is unstoppable in its momentum to advance in its quest to discover and experience more of itself.
Consider a child in school. Is there any limit to what her mind can absorb if her thirst for learning and knowledge is great? Of course not! There are not enough hours in her entire lifetime for that child to learn all that is available to learn in your reality. So it is the same with God's Universe. All experience is useful, even that which you deem to be negative! God does not judge or condemn anything, for He knows that much can be learned even from the most horrific mistakes.

In truth, some of the greatest lessons and healings have come from errors in human judgment that led to a change in consciousness. Is that not what one of your greatest teachers, Jesus came to demonstrate to the world? Yes, for Jesus came into the world knowing that He would be crucified and that His sacrifice would awaken mankind to the glory of God's love.

Q: What is the best healing modality to use?

God blessed the world with an array of healing modalities, to be as diverse as you are. In his infinite wisdom, He knew that what one of you might accept, another would reject. That is why your reality is varied and rich with choices. Yes, some of these modalities are more effective than others, but none are superior to the pure healing power of God's love when your fully awakened heart calls it forth.

The love that is God is the force that powers the Universe, it is the one eternal truth of all existence. All healing modalities are simply a human attempt to create a structure for you to harness that love in order to manifest a healing and alter your reality. The fact that these modalities can be successful is a testament to the Divine power that created you! But it is not the modality itself that heals.

A modality is useful to you only because your conscious mind has the need to focus on something external in order to believe it is real.

Your ego/logical mind requires form and structure to feel safe, but these are temporal and immaterial. In truth, you do not actually need a modality! *You* are the ultimate modality. The loving essence of the individual is what commands a healing in the Creator's name. Even the most unenlightened among you has the potential to experience a moment of Divine alignment with God that can manifest an instant healing! This is so because your true nature is love and on occasion, your ego-mind steps aside to let your God-ness shine through. That is why miracles can come to and through anyone.

The enlightened healer has learned how to set his lower ego/conscious mind aside to allow God's love to flow through him completely.

Q: How can I be sure that I am really talking to my angels?

Our communication with you has a unique feel and rhythm all of its own. Sometimes you may feel our loving presence strongly, other times you might feel nothing. Nevertheless, we assure you that we are always at your side, doing what we can to assist you without interfering with the lessons you have chosen to learn. Nothing is ever imposed upon you, for it would be a violation of Universal law. We can sometimes bend the laws, but we never break them.

Another way to tell if the messages are truly from the angels is quite simple: do the beings speak of God and openly praise Him? Or are the messages more generic and politically correct? The choice of words sometimes reflects the mindset and preferences of the channel himself. We say this to you because many leaders and teachers in the New Age seem uncomfortable using the word, "God." We understand that some prefer to not offend those who are Christian as well as those who are non-Christian, so they seek the middle road, the path of least offense. This choice is sometimes wise, but not always.

It is best to use the full power of a word to call forth and manifest what you desire.

It is with your thoughts and your words that you create anything and everything in your reality. A word has a vibration all its own, therefore some words have more intrinsic power than others. There is greater power in the words "God" or even "Allah," than in the word, "Source." Can you feel the difference in vibration? Choose your words wisely, and select them for their accumulated and inherent power, to manifest the highest good for all.

We serve God and our job is to lead you to Him—to lead you to yourself. Yes, work and communicate with us, but do not place us on a pedestal. You are equal to all conscious beings, to everything in the Universe. Even to the angels. You are also equal to God, because you ARE God. All of you have earned the right to work directly with the Creator, without an intermediary. The sequence of spiritual evolution is to seek God, then to surrender to God, and finally, become One with God.

Q: Why is there so much suffering on this planet?

Some of you have chosen to experience the illusion of separation from God's love. This can be one of the most challenging choices of all. It is like taking an advanced level college course instead of going into elementary school. When you see someone struggling with tremendous loss, illness, disease, or some other form of suffering, know that they deserve your compassion and support, but never your pity. Feeling pity for someone is disempowering since this energy is of such a low vibration. Choose instead to send them thoughts of hope, courage, and love. You do them no favor when you buy into someone's illusion of despair. Affirm what is positive instead, for in every tragic situation, there is always a seed of hope planted within.

All suffering is but a temporary misalignment in which the individual is disconnected from the God/love that they are.

This is the sacred path of the ascended masters who transcended their own human suffering on their way to spiritual ascension. All souls suffer who inhabit a body. For is your body not separate from your Divine spirit? Even as your consciousness creates your body, still the body is limited, since it is merely a vehicle for your spirit. You are not your body. Enjoy and celebrate your body while you are here, care for as it as your own sacred temple, but never worship the temple. It is only a temporary structure, whereas you are immortal.

Q: Do you have a closing message?

Some of you enjoy dabbling in spirituality and metaphysics because it makes you feel good and provides a respite from your daily struggles. Anything that spiritually uplifts you, we lovingly support. We simply wish to remind you that the planet needs all of you who are ready to embrace your destiny path, to do so without further delay. Those who have agreed to assist in the birthing of the Golden Age will feel a deep stirring within their heart when they read our words.

You have chosen the most amazing time to be alive!

Celebrate your present journey no matter how challenging it may be at the moment, for your reality can be altered positively in an instant. Begin each new day, lifting your heart and your mind higher. Let us help you connect to God. We share your destiny path, for we are walking it with you right now. So it is and always will be.

We are all one. You are God, as are we.

SONIA PASQUAL
VIOLETT FLAME
ORLANDO, FL

Sonia Pasqual Violett Flame is a spiritual teacher and guide, a Theta Healing Practitioner®, certified by Vianna Stibal, an ANGEL THERAPY PRACTITIONER®, certified by Doreen Virtue, Ph.D., a Reiki Master/Teacher, a crystal therapy practitioner, an intuitive consultant, and an ordained minister. Currently she is working on her master's degree in metaphysics from American Institute of Holistic Theology. Sonia enjoys helping people raise their consciousness to experience true happiness. Her passion is to coach and motivate anyone seeking the power of inner knowledge, living in joy, intuitive development, and enlightenment.

Sonia has developed and teaches many workshops. She is on the spiritual path of oneness for all. For more information about Sonia, visit her website, www.enlightenwithtruth.com, or email her at violettflame@yahoo.com.

Archangel Metraton Speaks

By Sonia Pasqual Violett Flame

You are a being of Divine love, which creates all things from within. Your core being has all the ingredients necessary to formulate truth and happiness. The world that you live in supports your creative process and life purpose. Earth's support structure, which aligns and brings all elements into balance, is sacred.

When I channeled this material, the energy that I was communicating with told me that its name was "Archangel Metraton." I have since discovered that Archangel Metraton is an alternate spelling for Archangel Metatron. Metraton, with assistance of other angels, has important information to share on the topics of Divine love, the collective consciousness, and sacred geometry.

Archangel Metraton says that as we reconnect with our higher selves and our Source, we can create a shift that brings us into alignment with who we really are. Sacred geometry, which is the use of geometric shapes and colors to solidify intentions and prayers, creates an aligned and balanced connection to being one with All That Is. It is through choice that we reconnect with the inner self or Divine love for great ascension. We have chosen to incarnate at this time for many reasons, all reasons leading to a greater purpose of existence. Archangels Metraton and Raziel have been working with me for some time now on sacred geometry and how it can be effective in our ascension process.

It is important to have a strong spiritual support structure in your life so that you can experience conscious growth and proceed along your enlightened path. The major component of a strong support structure is love. Love only comes from the Divine Source of All That Is. This love is not what we may conclude it to be from a human point of view. It is stronger, deeper, unconditional, and limitless. Archangel Metraton has channeled through me direction and guidance to create strong support structures that can help you reconnect to Divine love, the collective consciousness, DNA, and use of sacred geometry.

Divine love energy is transformative. The essence of Divine love is of oneness, wholesomeness, and truth. Its strong foundation is untouchable and unfathomable to the human conscious. Therefore, to acquire Divine love is to access the heart center by allowing the ego and third dimension of illusions to not be embraced any longer. This force of energy, that creates from deep within, may seem unreachable only because your mind may limit itself. There are no limits! This life force energy of Divine love is one with us because we are created from it. Therefore, you can reconnect to it by conscious decision to seek beyond any blocks of your human experiences. These experiences can be a pathway for you to direct this life force energy, this creative force in a positive and enlightening experience. Without this life force energy of love, no form of life has real purpose. All would be in vain and void! To exist and live in truth and happiness, the path of Divine love is the number one key to a strong support structure. Living in the present moment and allowing yourself to be connected to this Divine love allows you to be filled with life force energy to create and manifest. God surpasses all comprehension of life forces because this massive collective conscious is of the purest form that exists. You live in love, you live in true existence, and you then live in total, full abundance.

The collective consciousness is Divine love. All facultative of this Divine love is true. It can be accessed through dedication from the heart. The heart is the keyhole within each person that can access high vibration and accept it into Mother Earth's realm. Taking time to retreat by spending time in nature; for nature has not lost its full essence of being able to ground one's active mind and lessen the overloading of thinking. The outcome of connecting to Divine love will manifest great healings, unconditional love, happiness, peace, joy, and the New World shifts into the higher consciousness of the New Jerusalem, a new home, peace and livelihood for all. No more low vibrating conscious will exist or will there be lack, discrimination, suffering, pain, and illusions, for it will not able to survive. It is by choice to be in Divine love that will cause this successful shift to occur. The Archangel Metraton encourages us to play our role very well as the higher conscious and higher vibration that is needed for survival. To step away from ego and the illusions of the third dimension, that to see, feel, touch, hear and taste is the only real things; you will allow yourself the opportunity to discover beyond the human conscious mind and begin to access Divine love.

The collective conscious is healing, all-knowing, abundant, and flows at all times. It may be your mind that limits you and puts you outside this beautiful conscious existence. It cannot be said enough, that is only by choice that you can experience the truth and find real, everlasting happiness. A happiness that comes from experiencing truth from the Divine love and being in the collective conscious state. In this conscious state, the mind can learn to understand the importance and connection of love. The prerequisite to experience a deeper state of consciousness for truth, enlightenment, and growth is to come from and be in a place of love. The earth has housed much bloodshed, turmoil, hatred, and low energies, low esteem, guilt, fear, doubt, and worry. There needs to be a conscious shift, through our thoughts, energy, and love for a rebirth to take place and transit this low vibration and raise the vibration. The collective conscious can shift and raise the consciousness of any one part, including humanity, societies, communities, families, and all of Earth's inhabitants. As a whole form, a whole living entity Mother Earth and her inhabitants can raise vibration through a pure mind and heart. Therefore, all change starts within, then throughout into the Universe as a whole. For we are all one, under one collective conscious rule, we affect each other positively or negatively as a whole. It is through the collective consciousness that we build a strong support structure to All That Is. The Divine precedent or law is that of love, and love, through a conscious state.

The angels are a great assistance to the whole part of the collective conscious. They are here to be of service to our cause; the greater good is known to them. The Archangel Metraton raises consciousness from this collective Source to bring about wholesomeness as a high vibratory Source. Traveling through different existence of time and space, otherwise considered the present moment, this consciousness or Archangel has choose to give service of love for all involved. To be in service of love, one does not need to be in the spotlight, limelight or fame. Only the ego desires fame and paybacks. Archangel Metraton, once Enoch who was a servant for God, in service to help humanity throughout downfalls.

Archangel Metraton is part of the collective consciousness that chooses to help all through words, passion, love, and symbolic messages. Archangel Metraton and Archangel Raziel are assisting with restructuring all known sources necessary to help humanity and this planet back to prosperity of a fuller, higher consciousness. The human conscious is limited by illusions; these angelic beings are close to us for assisting. It is through the help of our angelic beings that we can choose to listen, reconnect to our higher purpose, and live in love and the collective conscious. This would help us each tap into our inner healer, lover, confidence, gifts, and creative manifesting. For it is Archangel Metraton's major role to spread the message of how to love. Now!

Archangel Metraton's guidance is to be prepared to go within oneself with practice, to listen and tap into your inner wisdom, let it flow outward. This inner wisdom is filled with the knowledge to educate oneself with one's mission and life purpose. This inner wisdom is flawless and full of truth. By the practice of going within, loving oneself, you will then be able to process and love another person. Your inner guidance system is ego-less, full of life force energy, direction, motivation, compassion, and brings you out of the illusions of grief or turmoil. This inner power is a source of love for transiting through life in general. As each individual goes within, with practice to listen, moving away from ego and the third-dimension illusions, we as a whole become stronger in many ways. The planet's consciousness will shift for greater purification, and great shifts will continue to happen one after the other.

The collective conscious, Archangel Metraton, and Archangel Raziel have to restructure the DNA of our cores to prepare for shift into this higher consciousness. This is part of the process; the DNA structures may have patterns that are no longer serving a purpose, but that of a lower vibration. The DNA can be renewed for a greater cause and effort for the higher vibration of consciousness. Since many of us cannot be reborn, this rebirthing is necessary for humanity. It affects us on all levels of our consciousness, reality, and being. There will be many forms of restructuring to help those enter into this high vibrational New World. There are many structures developed and developing. Examples are: Light Activation Healing System™ by Cindy Eyler, Theta Healing® by Vianna Stibal, and RaZiel Method of Healing System™ by Sonia Pasqual Violett Flame—all work on the DNA level and deep cellular healing. These systems work as an alternative healing, that works on the DNA, non-physical, and more complex human-spiritual anatomy, which create healings and high vibration of one's mind, body, and soul. Retrieving the soul fragments is necessary for full abundance and balance in one's life.

Archangel Metraton, Enoch of the I AM Presence, would like to tell the world how important it is to take care of itself. It is vital to set a structure of protection and love around you at all times. It is very important to know how we each affect each other and how we as individuals are united as one whole piece. Planet Earth is a piece of a Universal puzzle. Sacred geometry is comprised of shapes and symbols that are used to heighten a sense of being. You can, for example, visualize yourself in a triangle and see your conscious state being lifted to greater understanding. There are sacred geometric structures that create nature, leaves, trees, mountains, etc. on Earth. That is why being out in nature feels so grounding, natural, refreshing, and almost sacred, depending on where you are. The strongest support structure is the triangle. It has the ability to align and balance one's energy in terms of metaphysical therapies. Even architectural structures use triangle shapes as one of their strongest supports. Begin to view sacred geometry as a way for connecting to higher energies, having a strong support structure using sacred geometry, and connecting with nature in our daily lives for advancement in the higher conscious realm.

Call on the angels and give them permission to work with you in your life. Call on a particular angel, like Archangel Metraton, to fill your being with his restructuring for assisting you in forward motion to achieving higher vibration. It will take practice to go within and listen for your angels' guidance. The beauty of nature captivates each human soul in a form of some sort, allowing the person to experience the Divine love within them. You are able to love yourself more and hear your angelic guidance, receiving all the angelic messages that are full of joy, love, romance, self-love, inner peace, outer peace, fulfillment of all you truly desire, all you truly deserve to attain in this beautiful, conscious state of being. You are a deserving soul full of greatness, the vitality, and the zeal for life in itself. All is well, all is forever good as you allow your body to explore its inner knowledge, its inner being and powers that be; to reach into its inner depths and pull out the facets of life and happiness that deserves to be lived out in your earth's realm, your present state of being.

It is only the beginning of many great experiences. It is best to live it out in the greatness of one's beautiful grace and power to be in the present moment of happiness. The Archangel Metraton will not rest until each soul is retrieved and living in peace and harmony. It is the true, dedicated service of this angel to help all humanity prosper in the state of our collective consciousness. This angel will help us raise our standards of consciousness accordingly for success of each soul involved. There are no challenges in our existence, for each one has the angels, these Divine love assistants necessary for all higher vibrational change. Archangel Metraton assists the light young ones who are bringing and bridging the consciousness of planet Earth to a state of awareness.

There will be in families coming forth new consciousness, and as the population continues to grow, these light young ones will assist this archangel's mission and purpose for Mother Earth. Archangel Metraton's mission is of vibrating to a higher conscious state for success of this planet and its inhabitants. It is only through this higher state of consciousness can one exist and succeed to full potential in every cell of being know to man and God. It is the plan and the structure for survival. Archangel Metraton strives forward in excellence to bring about the renewal of great pure emotions not tainted by disappointments. Emotion full of true essence of life and love, emotion that is not weak to hold back one, but emotion strong in structure to be used as a driving force, an active role of one challenge to reach repurification of one's soul essence.

Going into one's core self through practice and discovering the true beauty of you will accomplish this re-purification. You have all the necessary ingredients within you to successfully create a new you that is deserving of the new energies to live in full happiness and abundance of this conscious state of being. It is for us to love this Universe in which we live and love the self, for it is the ultimate reward to our spiritual being. The first thing one should do upon waking is to love one self; it is a huge cause full of greatness for the body is the example of love itself. Every part of the body is an example of Divine pure love. One part to one part is a whole body full with love. This shift of consciousness to a greater cause is a true higher vibration for eternity.

Start with telling your body, "I love you." Feel this love within you and grow emotions of love that fills your being of light. Your light shines brightly, full of love, and each person's light will shine bright of a different glow in the spectrum of colors. At different times in life, different spectrums of colors will be seen for all equals to the purity of the soul. The essence of our being is the soul; the life force of our being is the Spirit within. We are all one in this mighty kingdom of Divine love, or oneness, or God. We are all a part of the same race united as one to push forward, conquering any low entity! We are strong! One being is a force of this light being, a piece of the puzzle, the strength of the chain. You are of Universal light, together forming a higher conscious-ness that which has never existed and forming a livelihood of existence that man has never been a part of and which only God has surpassed in thought form centuries ago. The time is now to shift in unison in this massive consciousness to experience bliss of wholesomeness together.

There is no need to do this alone or by one's self. A group effort is needed and will be formed at all times. There is a group conscious being formed in each part of society. It has been formed purposefully from the day of birth. You are of the Light! A consciousness unknown to humanity; a consciousness so developed and far beyond in greatness. The human race is ready, for the time is now to experience this dimension of reality by forming pieces upon the planet Earth. By the light within each being pulling pieces of this unique consciousness into Mother Earth's realm. Her womb is ready to be fertilized, for without it, she would perish and that should never happen, for it is not written that way by conscious design. Conscious design has a plan, a structure with massive forms of bliss for each one being involved. This consciousness is abundant in all aspects of time and reality, here and now, to shelter all of its inhabitants. The inhabitants are the human race, which is a part of this massive conscious mind. A whole is formed in the collective spectrum, and it is brightly shown in form, in structure, in humanity.

In conclusion to all that has been said, it is not our life's purpose to be in a place of pain or lack; it is only by our choice that we live in such conditions. Calling on one's angels for guidance, protection, and assistance can delete the harsh conditions experienced in life. The body is our temple of this eternal, Divine love. The mind is the essence of the strength of this eternal, Divine love. The soul is the foundation, the beauty, the dreamer and the doer, for all of life to succeed and be in the glorious, passionate love that can exist for each spiritual journey we experience as human beings. Love!

KIMBERLY KOLB
NASHVILLE, TN

K imberly Kolb holds a Bachelor of Science degree in Physical Therapy
and is a licensed physical therapist currently practicing as an ergonomic
consultant in the health care industry. She is a clairaudient spiritual coach and
energy healer who works with angels and ascended masters to facilitate
healing and spiritual growth in her clients.

Kim is an ANGEL THERAPY PRACTITIONER®, certified by Doreen
Virtue, Ph.D. In her free time, Kim can be found traveling the globe,
ballroom dancing, designing clothes, or fostering her newfound passion for
painting. You can contact Kim to schedule an appointment by emailing
voiceofangels@comcast.net, or visiting her website,
www.thevoiceofangels.com.

Spiritual Awakening

By Kimberly Kolb

I equate my spiritual transformation experience to awakening from a dream. When I look back at the unhappy person I was four years ago, it is hard to imagine that I am the same individual. As one who is deep in slumber, I was living in a dream state of negative reality created by my ego. I had lost sight of the Divine spark of light within me. My spiritual transformation was all about awakening from this ego-based dream, witnessing the Divine light within me, and remembering who I really am. God and the angels gently nudged me awake from that dream by giving me new opportunities to see the divine spark of light within. As my inner light began to sparkle brightly, I woke up and started on a new course with a renewed sense of passion.

Four years ago, before my spiritual awakening, I worked as an ergonomic consultant and physical therapist at a local hospital. I was in a helping profession—I should have felt fulfilled and effective in my work. Instead, I was bored, angry, and anxious to leave. *What's wrong with me?* I wondered sadly. Deep inside, I knew I no longer felt inspired to do hospital work. I had no idea how to recapture the sense of enthusiasm I felt when I first began my career.

I was also drifting away from the church of my childhood. I attended services faithfully and was in the church choir. I'd known many of the congregants all of my life. I was thoroughly indoctrinated in the ways of the Christian tradition. And yet, as I sat in the choir loft on any given Sunday, I felt utterly bored, disconnected, and separated from God. The sermon messages escaped me, and often I realized I had "checked out" both mentally and spiritually during the service.

I also struggled with the inconsistencies observed between word, deed, and church politics that forced congregants and church leaders to make choices against their consciences. I saw well-meaning Christians choosing actions from a place of fear and hatred instead of from love, as Jesus taught us.

I had a strong feeling that my perceptions were valid and real—I was seeing the ugly side of religion, and it scared me. But I felt powerless to do anything about it.

Please know that it is not my intent to malign or ridicule churches of the Christian tradition in any way—I believe there are many paths to God. During my personal journey, however, I realized that the church of my upbringing was no longer my path to God.

One Sunday after church I was sitting in my car in the church parking lot, thinking *I just can't do this anymore. I am bored and unfulfilled worshiping here.* I felt fear welling up in my stomach at the thought of leaving the church. Just then I heard a firm and loving male voice say, "Dearest Kim, it is time for you to leave. It is safe for you to go."

I had no idea where the disembodied voice came from. I even doubted that I'd really heard anything. Nonetheless, I laughingly answered, "Yeah, right. And go where?"

The voice replied, "You will know when you find it."

I burst into tears, afraid and frustrated. I had sole responsibility—it was up to me to choose whether to stay or to go. I felt so scared and alone, separated from God, and now, I was destined to leave the only religion I'd ever known.

Looking back, I believe the Holy Spirit spoke to me that day, either directly or through the voice of an angel.

I was finally being nudged awake, out of the dream and into the truth.

The search for a new church was not as quick or easy as I wanted it to be. I remember asking aloud, "What church should I visit?" expecting *The Voice* to give me a straight-forward answer that would swiftly and efficiently tell me the right church to attend. Instead, I heard nothing. Once again, I was over-whelmed by feelings of isolation and fear.

But I wasn't alone—God was working in mysterious ways, sending me guidance in the forms of angels, human beings acting as "Earth angels," and many synchronistic events.

As I visited church after church in search of a spiritual home, one of my coworkers suggested I try the local Unity church. He told me the church had a great music director and a gospel choir. That part sounded good to me, but I was scared of the unknown, afraid that Unity was a cult.

Shortly after my coworker made his suggestion, I attended a workshop for Nashville Diversity in Dialogue, an organization that formed dialogue groups to discuss racism and develop proactive community responses. During this workshop, we discussed visiting churches outside of our comfort zone to foster understanding of different cultures and religions. A woman from the group encouraged me to visit her place of worship, Unity. Okay, that was the second time I'd heard of this church. I was beginning to suspect that it wasn't a coincidence.

Later that spring, I was thumbing through the local health and wellness magazine. The publication fell open to a page with many churches listed on it. My eye was drawn to the advertisement for the Unity church.

Now my curiosity was piqued. I had to visit this church. I do not believe these three events were unconnected or random coincidences. I believe that angels and earth angels were dispatched from God to send me a message, to guide me on my search for a new church home.

I walked into the Unity church sanctuary and found a seat at the end of a row, near the back—I figured I could make a quick escape if things got too weird for me. Soon, however, I was at ease. Everything from the eloquent grand piano music and the centered meditation time, to the warm welcoming by congregants filled my senses with a feeling of peace. At one point, the minister said to all visitors, "We believe you are not here by accident, but rather by Divine appointment." Those words, as well as the words in the daily message, felt true to me. I had a sense that the message was being spoken directly to me. It was as if God was whispering in my ear, "You found it! You are home now!"

Within six months, I'd made Unity my new church home, joined the choir, and made several spiritually like-minded friends. It is amusing to me that some of the opportunities we strongly resist in life are the very experiences that we need to grow and prosper on our journey.

Finding a new spiritual home was just the start of my transformational process. Many of the friendships made at Unity have led to significant spiritual discoveries. One of my new church friends frequently encouraged me to broaden my spiritual understanding. She invited me to visit local New Age stores and attend holistic fairs—experiences far outside the narrow boundaries of my Christian-oriented comfort zone. My instinct was to approach these visits with much skepticism and caution. One oppressively hot and humid July afternoon, we visited my first New Age Expo held in an older shopping mall that had seen better days. We came to a booth that advertised angel readings. I'd never had a psychic reading before, but I figured that a reading from the angels couldn't get me into too much trouble. When it was my turn to talk to the angel reader, I was anxious and fearful; yet some inner guidance pushed me to proceed. In my center, I knew that I was safe and that I might learn something important.

Nothing could have prepared me for what I experienced during this angel reading. The reader started with a short prayer of protection while we held hands. She commented that things felt different for her. She usually had to close her eyes and go within to hear the voice of one or two angels who wanted to communicate with her clients. But with me, her eyes were open, and she initially had trouble hearing one clear message because there was a room full of angels, all crowding around me, all excitedly talking at once. These are the messages the reader channeled from the angels:

"You are one of us; you are an angel of such high order and frequency. You came to earth to provide healing."

"You can both be part of this world and acknowledge your heavenly heritage."

"The spirit of God is working through you."

"There is work for you to do as your angel self to help change the vibration of those around you."

"A new earthly teacher is coming into your life to guide you and help you open to new levels of awareness."

"We love you so much. We are now sending forth an energy that is so strong and powerful that you will feel it in your physical body and you will know how much we love you."

I experienced a huge shift of energy in my heart and solar plexus—it felt like love was filling all the empty spaces within me. It was a warmth and compassion beyond measure. The depth of emotion experienced at this moment made both the angel reader and me cry. Needless to say, this was quite an initiation to communicating with the angelic realm, and I was stunned!

After the reader finished channeling the angels, she suggested that I read some books written by Doreen Virtue. While I was rather unsure about the validity of all the messages I'd just received, I figured it would not hurt to at least read some books about angels. I chose to read Doreen's book, *Divine Guidance: How to Have a Dialogue With God and Your Guardian Angels.* While the concepts she described in the book sounded good in print, I knew that I would need more personal instruction to fully understand and practice Divine, angelic communication. I searched Doreen's website to learn more about her and her work with angels. Concurrently, I was learning the concept of synchronicity from other prominent authors such as Deepak Chopra and James Redfield, who had given talks at the Unity church. I understood that nothing happens by accident or coincidence. All events are part of a larger plan that we put into motion with our thoughts. Therefore, I knew it was no accident that Doreen was giving a workshop based on her book, *Earth Angels*, in two months, on my birthday! I was so intrigued by this discovery that I decided to attend this workshop in Sedona, Arizona.

A few days later, two acquaintances from Unity independently initiated a conversation with me mentioning Sedona. I'd never even heard of the destination before that week—I believe the angels were trying to get my attention and sent messages through these friends to confirm that I was on the right track. I did extensive Internet research to learn more about Sedona and found that it has quite the reputation as *the* Spiritual Mecca of North America. I became engrossed in the lore of the area and made my travel plans—absent-mindedly forgetting to purchase tickets to the *Earth Angels* workshop itself!

Once I got to Sedona, I was on a nature hike with a local guide, and she casually mentioned to me that a famous angel expert was giving a talk at the educational center the next day. I slapped the side of my head and said, "Are you talking about Doreen Virtue?" The guide confirmed this was the author who would be speaking to a sold-out audience. Meanwhile, I was punishing myself for being so stupid as to forget to buy tickets in advance. The guide said, "The workshop is sold out, but I think you should go early and stand in line anyway. I get a strong feeling that you are supposed to be there, and you will get in."

I doubted her advice at the time, thinking, *This is just woo-woo Sedona talk*. Then again, what did I have to lose?

I arrived at the workshop location one hour early and stood in the long entrance line. The lady standing behind me in line had a bright tangerine-orange top on. Although I typically dislike the color orange, I thought the woman's top was genuinely pretty. For some unknown reason, I turned around and told her how much I liked her blouse. We struck up a conversation, and I mentioned that she could go ahead of me because I did not have a ticket and probably would not get in. She said, "Oh, I may be able to help you with that. My friend bought a ticket and cannot come. You could buy her ticket."

How could I ever doubt the existence of angels and divine guidance after this obvious turn of events in my favor? I was clearly supposed to attend the *Earth Angels* workshop.

entered the hall and sat next to a well-seasoned group of angel lovers whose mannerisms and discussion topics felt very foreign to me. When Doreen Virtue came on the stage and invoked the archangels in meditation, there was a palpable energy shift in the room. I felt a cool breeze across my face and arms. This, too, felt foreign and unexplainable. Doreen taught there are different types of angels. The archangels like Michael, Raphael, Gabriel, and Uriel are of a higher station and oversee the functions of guardian angels. We also learned that each person has at least one guardian angel who is with us from birth to death. Their function is to assist us with day-to-day tasks when we ask them, and to intervene should we encounter a life-threatening situation before it is our time to transition. Doreen spoke in detail about her book *Earth Angels*, describing the common characteristics of each group. During the class, I received confirmation of all that had been told me in the angel reading just months earlier.

Over the next year, I read every book I could find on angels and began to hear that still, small inner voice telling me to get further training. Against the financial odds of being downsized at work, I manifested the funds to attend Doreen's ANGEL THERAPY PRACTITIONER® training. During our training, we cleared many of the fears that blocked us from receiving angelic guidance. We learned to use these innate psychic, intuitive skills to guide and heal others. I received a clear message from the angels that my life purpose is to heal others through intention, presence, and touch. The angels said that earthly teachers would be sent to help me remember how to use my God-given healing gifts.

Just as the angels foretold, I was led to study with three different energy healers over the next year. I gained knowledge and experience from learning each technique; however, I strongly resonated with the simple and effective healing modality developed by Richard Gordon called Quantum Touch. In this hands-on healing method, the practitioner uses breathing techniques, focused intention, and circulation of life-force energy to create an atmosphere in which the client's body heals itself. As I learned these healing techniques, I got a vision of God and the angels working through me to heal others. I often experienced the cool, etheric presence of angels moving through me during a healing session. Clients frequently report the same feeling of Divine love energy filling their body during a healing session. I could finally see with clarity and feel with certainty how I was to fulfill my life purpose healing and serving others.

But my spiritual transformation was not complete. The angels led me to remember another vital piece of information that would impact every area of my life—the transformative powers of positive thought and affirmation. Despite reconnecting with God and the angels and discovering my life's purpose, I continued to encounter difficult situations at the hospital and felt limited by a lack of financial abundance. The angels led me to study the Law of Attraction and to learn the power of my thoughts and words. They sent an avalanche of knowledge on the subject in the form of movies, CDs, and books. The Law of Attraction, a quantum physics principle highlighted in the movies *What the Bleep do we Know?* and *The Secret*, explains the energetic connection between our thoughts and words and the events that occur around us. Many recently published books detail how to use affirmations to create the life of your dreams. Once I began to see how rapidly my words and thoughts manifested into reality, I realized that I had created the problematic situations at work and the illusion of financial lack. I learned to stop the ripple of negativity from spreading into my reality by immediately counteracting it with a positive affirmation. My new understanding of the Law of Attraction and the power of affirmations has transformed my professional interactions and experiences at the hospital. In the past year I fulfilled my dream to travel to Hawaii, Australia, and New Zealand. This would not have been possible without turning around my beliefs of financial lack to affirmations and beliefs of infinite abundance.

When I look back at the path I've traveled in just a few short years, I am amazed by the depth of growth and transformation that has occurred. I no longer feel separate or alone in the world; I am comforted by my new spiritual awareness. My spiritual practices have built a strong bridge connecting me with the voice of God and the angels. I use God-given angelic skills to effect positive changes and healing for myself and those around me. Thank you, angels, for guiding me on this transformative journey, leading me back into relationship with God, and showing me how to fulfill my earthly mission.

CAROLYN KELLIS REED
MERCED, CA

Cover artist Carolyn Kellis Reed is a clairvoyant medium with a special interest in the healing aspects of mediumship between dimensions. It is her honor and privilege to connect those who live on Earth with those who have departed this world, so that both parties may experience reconciliation and peace.

Carolyn also works internationally as an integral life coach. She skillfully combines her business background, intuition, coaching training, and knowledge of energetic healing modalities to assist her clients in leading healthier and more balanced, heart-centered lives.

Carolyn is an ANGEL THERAPY PRACTITIONER®, certified by Doreen Virtue, Ph.D., is a Reiki Master, is a certified medium, and is certified as an Integral Coach through New Ventures West, in San Francisco. She holds a BA and MBA from the University of California and is a former bank executive and business consultant. She is currently completing her Ph.D. dissertation in holistic ministries through the American Institute of Holistic Theology.

She has five bright and beautiful children, and lives with her husband Frank in Merced, California. She enjoys travel, reading, and joyful art creation with watercolor. She can be reached at carolyn.reed@yahoo.com.

MALACHITE PRESS

About Malachite Press

Malachite Press seeks to be of service by helping authors publish books that help make the world a better place. Focusing on metaphysical, spiritual, religious, inspirational, and self-help books, Malachite Press experts offer a comprehensive list of services to help authors' dreams come true. For more information about Malachite Press, call (800) 798-9270 or visit www.malachitepress.com.